MW01141720

# REAL PEOPLE *with*
# REAL STRATEGIES *for*
# REAL ESTATE INVESTING

Copyright © 2010 by Rick McKinnon and Leslie Quinsay.

All rights reserved. This book may not be reproduced in whole or in part, by any means, without written consent of the publisher. For permission requests, write to the publisher, addressed "Attention: Permissions Coordinator" at the address below.

THE ULTIMATE PUBLISHING HOUSE (TUPH)
US HEADQUARTERS
The Ultimate Publishing House (TUPH)
P.O. Box 1204
Cypress, Texas, U.S.A. 77410

49540 – 80 GLEN SHIELDS AVENUE, TORONTO, ONTARIO
CANADA, L4K 2B0

Telephone: 647.883.1758 Fax: 416-228-2598
www.ultimatepublishinghouse.com  and www.R3book.com

US OFFICE: Ordering Information

Quantity Sales: COMPANIES, ORGANIZATIONS, INSTITUTIONS, AND INDUSTRY PUBLICATIONS:
Quantity discounts are available on bulk purchases of this book for reselling, educational purposes, subscription incentives, gifts, sponsorship, or fundraising. Unique books or book excerpts can also be fashioned to suit specific needs such as private labelling with your logo on the cover and a message or a message printed on the second page of the book.  For more information please contact our Special Sales Department at The Ultimate Publishing House.

Orders for college textbook / course adoption use.
Please contact the Ultimate Publishing House
Tel: 647 883 1758

**TUPH** is a registered trademark of The Ultimate Publishing House

This book is not intended to provide legal, accounting, investing, or financial advice. Readers are encouraged to seek the counsel of proficient professionals with regard to such matters as interpretations of the law, accurate investment strategies, financial planning and accounting procedures. The Authors and Publisher specifically disclaim any liability, loss or risk which is incurred as a consequence, directly or indirectly, of the use and application of any of the contents of this work.

PRINTED IN CANADA

*R3: Real People with Real Strategies for Real Estate Investing*
by Rick McKinnon and Leslie Quinsay.
ISBN: 978-0-9819398-5-8

# RICK MCKINNON & LESLIE QUINSAY

## REAL PEOPLE *with*
## REAL STRATEGIES *for*
## REAL ESTATE INVESTING

*Developing the Mindset for Success*

4

# *Leslie's Acknowledgements*

To my parents, Armando and Elisa Lopez, who have been constant sources of inspiration, support, and encouragement throughout my entire life. I have learned so much, not only from the things you make an effort to teach me, but mostly from the examples you have set in every area of my life. All of my success has been possible because of the foundation you set for me. You are my greatest mentors.

To my son, Ethan, who keeps me young and motivates me more than anyone else in the world. Thank you for teaching me to see the world from such a positive and refreshing perspective. You remind me that, in the end, we are all children at heart.

To my husband, Ron, who has always supported and encouraged me to pursue my dreams. Thank you for always being there and for the sacrifices you have made so that I could work toward building my real estate investment business.

To the rest of my immediate and extended family. Thank you for keeping me focused on the bright side of things and pushing me forward when I didn't think I could push any farther. As a team, we've always been able to accomplish so much and propel each other toward our individual successes.

To my closest friends, Tanya Skaljac, Seema Patel, Abigail Alejandro-Mamaril, and Grace Marquez. You are all such strong, independent women who I respect and admire for your positive attitudes and never-ending support and enthusiasm. I am so grateful to have been able to ride the ups and downs of this roller coaster called life in both business and life experiences with each of you.

To Felicia Pizzonia and the entire team at TUPH. Thank you for all of your help and guidance in making the publication of our first book a reality. It has truly been a pleasure working with you.

5

And last, but definitely not least, to Rick McKinnon, one of my dearest friends, business associates, and co-author of this book. From the day we met, I knew that there must have been a reason you came into my life. Thank you for being such an enthusiastic and positive source of inspiration and focus. Working together on this book and building our businesses has been and will continue to be an adventurous journey. I'm truly grateful that we are able to share in it together.

# *Rick's Acknowledgements*

To my parents, Robert and Beverley Mckinnon, whose love and support throughout my life is the reason all of this was possible. Dad, your strength and guidance taught me to be strong and determined and that I could achieve anything in life. Mom, I still can't believe you're gone and not a day goes by that I don't miss you. Although you couldn't be here with me to share my accomplishment in writing this book, you are always in my heart. The love you showed for your family is what inspired me to be so passionate and focused in everything I do. I dedicated this book to you, Mom. I couldn't have accomplished it without you.

To my family, Jon, Jennifer, and Jeffrey, who have always encouraged me to follow my dreams and believed in me and what I could accomplish. To my brothers, Terry, Tim, and Steve, who I had the best childhood memories growing up with. Steve, we have always been close and supported each other in every way and you are not only my brother but my closest friend.

To Leslie Quinsay, business associate and co-author of this book. You have proven to be a great inspiration for me, not only in business but in my personal life. I admire your energy, enthusiasm, focus, and positive attitude. From the first day we met, you have supported and encouraged me to succeed in growing my portfolio as well as becoming one of my closest friends.

To Felicia Pizzonia and the entire team at TUPH. Thank you for all your help and guidance in making the publication of our first book a reality. It has truly been a pleasure working with you.

WWW.R3BOOK.COM

# R3 Table of Contents

WWW.R3BOOK.COM

10

# *Introduction*

Welcome and congratulations on taking the first step toward building a solid, profitable real estate portfolio! The information and stories contained within *R3: Real People with Real Strategies for Real Estate Investing* will help you to move forward in achieving your real estate investment goals. Whether you are just getting started or already have several properties under your belt, you will find many helpful lessons throughout each chapter.

We provide you with Canadian examples of an international process that gets results. With our proprietary strategy, you can successfully evaluate any property, anywhere in the world. Our success, and the success of our corporate clients, proves that this strategy works.

We urge you to read the entire book, rather than skimming its pages. Each chapter highlights a segment of our successful, step-by-step process. In addition, each chapter contains guidance on developing the crucial mindset for success. We know that creating wealth through real estate investing requires such a mindset, and this book is crafted around this vital principle.

When you picked up this book, you took action toward becoming a successful, sophisticated real estate investor. Why? Because you took the time to invest in your greatest asset: you! Truly successful individuals know that this is the only asset that can never be lost. Your talent and skill remain with you throughout the upswings and downturns that are part of every economic cycle. They help you to succeed, no matter what is happening in the marketplace. Fortunes are made, lost, and remade on a regular basis; you may lose money, property, and material goods, but no one can take away your knowledge.

Positive-minded opportunity seekers will always thrive in every economy, including the restructuring occurring today. *Canadian Business* magazine reported that, in 2009, there were

55 billionaires in Canada, up from 53 in 2008, and the total net worth of the richest 100 was $172.7 billion, up from $165.1 billion in 2008. Clearly, the rich are growing richer. T. Harv Eker, author of *Secrets of the Millionaire Mind*, said, "I don't claim to know what's going to happen in the economy, but I frankly don't really care. I'm going to take advantage of whatever is going on. You focus on what you want."

Investing in your skill helps you to continuously build and rebuild wealth for yourself. Success means learning from your mistakes, and building upon those mistakes instead of dwelling on them. The wealthiest people in the world realize that, no matter what circumstances arise, they are able to see beyond any obstacles and take the steps necessary to rise to the top—time and time again in any economy. They invest in themselves and are continuously building their skill at creating and maintaining their wealth.

If you read this book, clearly define your goals, and take action by implementing the lessons you learn, then you will be well on your way to creating a secure, lasting financial foundation. Commit to spending time absorbing and understand the information we have presented, but most importantly, start taking action! As Conrad Hilton says, "Success seems to be connected with action. Successful people keep moving. They make mistakes, but they don't quit."

This book is based on our experiences in real estate investing. It is not intended to be a scholarly textbook with rigid, step-by-step procedures. We teach, first and foremost, from our position as successful real estate investors. This book is designed to motivate you while teaching by example. We show you the good, the bad, and the ugly from what we have personally experienced.

This book was written with the understanding that we all learn in different ways. Your path to success may be vastly different from ours, but regardless of how success is achieved, there are always lessons to be learned. We hope to accelerate your success by sharing our challenges and helping you to avoid some of the mistakes we made when we began.

We also want to promote financial literacy and wealth creation and build a network of like-minded individuals. We feel that, by sharing with others in a spirit of cooperation rather than competition, we will propel each other toward success. Our goal is to help plant the seeds of a healthy financial foundation for as many people as possible.

**Find an Inspiring Mentor**

To be successful, you don't have to reinvent the wheel. Just figure out what you want to do and then turn to those who are already successful at doing it. Seek out a mentor who is willing to share his or her experience with you. Having someone to guide you through the obstacles is one of the most efficient ways to achieve success. In this way, you can stand on the shoulders of giants.

Having a mentor doesn't necessarily mean face-to-face meetings; it can be as simple as reading a book by someone you admire. We enjoy reading books by successful people such as Donald Trump and Robert Kiyosaki. Not only do their books motivate us, the challenges they faced give us the strength to get through our own obstacles, which suddenly seem a lot smaller.

A large part of our success has come from the advice and guidance of our mentors. We thought the best way to honor this, and show our gratitude, was to share our process and experience with other potential investors through this book and the seminars we hold. Our mentors helped us to achieve phenomenal success; we hope, in turn, to give you a head start toward building your own successful real estate portfolio.

**Leslie Talks About Working With Rick**

Looking back, I can see that, whenever I reached a turning point or crossroads in my life, the right person or opportunity always showed up to help guide me through it. Whether it was a friend, a mentor, a course, or an inspiring book, it seemed to appear at just the right time. As the saying goes, "When the

student is ready, the teacher will appear." It's amazing how, when the right people come into your life, you are able to feed off each other's positive, motivating energy.

The synergy that comes from surrounding yourself with like-minded individuals is amazing. It allows you to grow and succeed much faster than if you tried to go it alone. It's as though you propel each other toward success by constantly pushing, encouraging, and motivating each other.

A large part of my more recent success comes from the synergy between me and my business partner, Rick. Through working together, I've achieved some of my greatest goals and I'm truly grateful for that.

A few years back, Rick owned a company that specialized in restoration and renovation. I came by to view one of his properties and we were introduced through a mutual friend. Aside from the obligatory "Hi, it's nice to meet you," there was nothing more to it. But a few months later, I was having some issues with repair work on a few of my Edmonton, Alberta properties, and Rick's years of firsthand experience helped me tremendously. While working together, we discovered our shared passion for entrepreneurship and real estate.

Back in Ontario, we began meeting regularly to talk over our plans, share business ideas, and discuss real estate investing in general. I was considering investing in Hamilton, Ontario but wasn't familiar with the area. Since Rick lived there, he showed me around, explaining the different neighborhoods in the city. He described the economic fundamentals that made Hamilton a great place to invest. His insights gave me the confidence to start analyzing some properties.

Eventually, Rick pushed me to put in some offers on the most promising real estate investments. The first two offers did not produce results. But we were successful in purchasing a 30,000-square-foot office building. In addition to providing rental income, it is now the site of our corporate offices.

It isn't often that you meet someone who understands what you are trying to achieve and shares your vision, passion, and positive outlook on life. We will sit for hours, debating the pros and cons of our different ideas. There is always so much excitement and passion about how we are trying to achieve our business goals. Even though we don't always agree, we take the time to respectfully hear each other out.

Sometimes, after arguing back and forth, we end up in agreement. More often, after much heated debate, we just end up agreeing to disagree. That's one of the things I like best about our working relationship. We have strong opinions and aren't afraid to voice them; at times our opinions will conflict, but we always respect each other's point of view.

When I had to make some difficult decisions about several personal issues, it was Rick who pushed me to make the right choices and take action. He challenged me every step of the way. I knew in the back of my mind that he was right, but was afraid to move forward. I found a million reasons not to act. He expressed a genuine desire to help me succeed and got me out of my comfort zone.

Over the course of a year we collaborated on a few projects in the Kitchener-Waterloo, Ontario area. Then we began developing larger, more creative strategies for building long-term wealth. Our confidence grew out of fully supporting and encouraging each other to move past our fears and take the necessary action. We didn't allow each other time to hesitate and ponder what could go wrong. We challenged each other to remain focused on what we were trying to accomplish. We reminded each other that, although there would invariably be mistakes along the way, as long as we were moving forward there would always be progress.

It was during this time that Rick's mom began her fatal struggle with cancer. Looking back, I'm amazed at how he managed to take care of his parents, his family, and his day-to-day life while remaining so positive and focused on his business ideas. Maybe it was the inspiration his mom provided; maybe it's just a natural part of who he is. But at a time when most people fall apart, Rick stepped up to the plate and did what had to be done.

There wasn't much I could do to help so I just tried to be the best friend I could be and listened when he needed to vent. I learned a lot from the example Rick set during this difficult time in his life. I am glad that I could be there to support and encourage him as he worked through it.

Over the past few years we have both enjoyed phenomenal success; it is the fortunate result of the synergy from working together. Today, we continue to collaborate in building our individual real estate portfolios and consulting businesses. In addition, we have co-authored this book to motivate and inspire other potential investors because this is what we are passionate about. Real estate investing is helping us to create the abundance and wealth we want in our lives.

We urge you to discover what part of this industry fires your passion, and then create the right mindset for success. Believe in yourself and your ability to reach your goals, and then nothing will be able to stop you.

# Chapter One

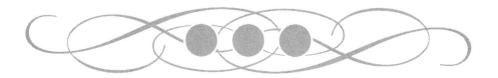

## *Property Passion:*

### THE MANY REWARDS OF REAL ESTATE INVESTING

Most people begin with the question, "What should I invest in?" But in *R3: Real People with Real Strategies for Real Estate Investing*, you will find that the more important question to ask is, "What am I trying to accomplish by investing?" If you do not have an end result clearly fixed in your mind, it can be confusing and difficult to determine what type of investment works best for you and how best to accomplish your goal.

Our proven, proprietary strategy helps you to create wealth through real estate investing. But real estate investing must tie into your long-term goals and dreams, and you must have a very clear sense of purpose. This will help you to stick with it through the inevitable bumps along the road.

In our seminar, we found that it is a very valuable exercise for people to sit down and answer this question at length. We recommend that you find a quiet hour in which to do the same. What do you truly hope to accomplish through real estate investing? Your answers may surprise you.

For some people, it can provide financial freedom when they retire, offering passive income to support their desired lifestyle. For others, it is about supporting their family, creating long-term wealth with tangible assets, and passing these assets on from generation to generation. Understanding your reason will help you to keep your sights on your target while building your portfolio.

We all have different objectives and motivations for investing in real estate. But your purpose for doing so should include developing the positive, optimistic mindset that spells success in this industry. It includes thinking like an entrepreneur: staying focused; being proactive; devising creative strategies to achieve your goal; and having an 'ownership' mentality where you are accountable for everything that goes on within your portfolio. Read Chapter Two for more information about developing the right mindset for success.

In addition to having a clear, specific understanding of where you want to be in several years, establishing a baseline of where you are today will help you to develop your action plan. Evaluating the gap—between where you are right now and where you want to be—is the only way to truly measure progress as you continuously build your portfolio. Remember that success is a journey; it is important to value each obstacle you have overcome and celebrate each milestone you accomplish.

**What Wealth Means to Rick**

I measure wealth in two ways: first, in financial abundance, and second, but most importantly, in the ability to provide for

my family. I take great pride in the fact that I have been successful as a real estate investor. But I am even more proud that my success allows me to care for the most important thing in my life: my family.

My father suffered from Alzheimer's and dementia for years, but my mother refused to place him in a retirement home. With the assistance of home health care workers, and despite having a full-time job, she continued to care for my father in their own home until she became very ill. Diagnosed with lung cancer in April 2008, she was determined to not let the disease interfere with her loving care of her family. Throughout her chemo and radiation treatments, she was in pain but kept her outlook positive; she was far more concerned about how it affected her family than about herself.

At this point, Leslie and I purchased my parents' house, making all mortgage and property tax payments, so that she could continue to live there for free. I felt great pride in being able to do this. I helped my mother to enjoy the time she had left without worrying about mortgage payments or bills. Wealth in this case meant the ability to give my mother a sense of pride and help her enjoy the time she had left.

When buying real estate, it's not always about making money. It can also be about the ability to help family when they need you the most. And sometimes it's about the freedom to support a friend in need. Leslie never hesitated in purchasing my parents' home to help my mother, despite the fact that she could lose money in the transaction. Leslie's caring, kindness, and support showed my mother, and my entire family, that she is a very special person.

### The Many Benefits of Real Estate

There are many excellent reasons why real estate should be a fundamental part of your investment portfolio:

- Three profit centers: appreciation, rental income, and mortgage principal reduction
- Leverage increases your investment
- Enjoy direct control over your asset
- Tangible assets can be developed in many ways
- Long-term, intergenerational wealth is possible
- The market moves slowly, allowing you time to adjust your strategy
- Portfolio diversification enhances the overall value

### The Three Profit Centers

In most cases, when people think about real estate and its potential return, they only consider how its value can appreciate over time. However, one benefit of including income-producing real estate in your investment portfolio is that there are three profit centers: appreciation, rental income, and mortgage principal reduction. When you take them all into account, you will realize that your return is likely higher than originally anticipated.

### *Profit Center One: Appreciation*

The *Dictionary of Real Estate Terms* from Barron's Business Guides  defines appreciation as "an increase in the value of property. Causes of appreciation for real estate may include inflation, demand pressures for land and buildings, a physical addition, modernization, removal of a negative factor from within or outside a property, and sweat equity ." While inflation is a passive factor over which you as an investor have little control, you can directly influence all other factors mentioned in this definition.

By following the steps and advice in this book, our proprietary strategy will ensure that your investment property is carefully selected to profit from appreciation. This process begins with a thorough property analysis, including assessing the area within which it is located (see Chapter Five). This will ensure that demand pressures for land and buildings will lead to an increase in their value. It will also help identify any negative factors within or outside the property that, by removing them, will lead to an increase in its value.

In Chapter Six, you will learn about the value of preparing a detailed repair-cost plan. For example, you will know in advance what modifications, such as an addition, will offer the greatest increase in value for your property. Costing out the work can also help you to compare the expense of hiring a contractor versus investing your own time, or sweat equity, into repairs.

The following charts illustrate how real estate investments typically appreciate over time. These charts apply to American and Canadian real estate, but the same holds true for other regions in the world. Although the market is cyclical, as is the case with most other forms of investment, real estate values generally continue to trend upward.

In addition, as you will learn in Chapter Three, with a leveraged investment the effect of appreciation is multiplied. The dollar value of your investment becomes much higher than the actual cash you utilized to acquire it.

## Average House Prices for Single-Family Homes
## Greater Toronto Area (Canada)

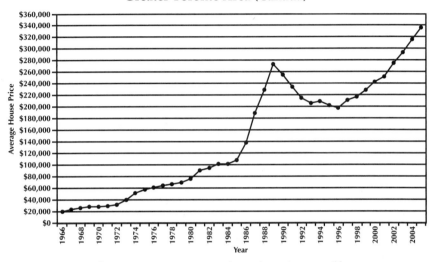

*Source: www.census.gov/const/uspriceann.pdf*

## Average Price of New Homes Sold in United States

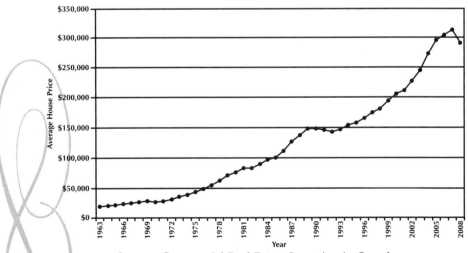

*Source: Commercial Real Estate Investing in Canada*
*Pierre Boiron, Claude Boiron*
*John Wiley & Sons Canada, Ltd. 2008*

### Profit Center Two: Rental Income

A carefully chosen, income-producing real estate portfolio will generate steady rental income. The key is ensuring that your properties are located in areas with strong economic fundamentals for future growth, a strong rental market base, and low vacancy rates. In addition, it is important to keep your properties well maintained and managed to attract quality tenants.

To stay competitive, you must market any vacant rental units as soon as they become empty to protect this source of income. Most people use standard advertising methods such as newspaper classifieds, free Internet sites, and flyers posted in local stores. However, if you can think "outside the box" with new and creative ways to advertise and show your properties, this can greatly enlarge your pool of potential tenants. For example, in our advertising we offer a $100 gift certificate upon the signing of a one-year lease. It is a small investment to make to entice qualified potential tenants. It also stands out if your ad is among several other similar properties available for rent. Remember, good tenants will take care of your property and pay you monthly rent that should be adequate to cover your operating expenses and debt service on the property. A small token such as the $100 gift certificate shows them that you are a landlord who cares about and respects the landlord-tenant relationship.

Keep in mind that your goal is positive cash flow, in which your rental income is more than enough to cover the property's operating costs and debt service (see Chapter Six). Careful planning will ensure this occurs; otherwise, you will be putting cash into your property month after month to cover an unplanned shortfall.

### Profit Center Three: Mortgage Principal Reduction

When this positive cash flow is achieved, your financial costs are covered in two ways: the interest is tax deductible and your rental income covers your mortgage payments and operating costs.

Your interest costs are tax deductible: Each month, you make payments to your lender on the mortgage covering your investment property. This debt service is a combination of the interest accruing on the initial loan and the actual repayment of the principal, or loan. In Canada and the United States, you can write off the interest payments because your property is a real estate investment. Therefore, even though you are receiving rental income, the amount of your taxable income is reduced. Although the proprietary R3 strategy is effective at evaluating any property, anywhere in the world, different tax laws can apply; check the laws in the country you are considering investing in as part of your property research.

Your tenants pay your mortgage: By ensuring that your investment property is continually rented, you ensure that a positive cash flow will cover your monthly mortgage payment as well as related property expenses. So, at the end of the day, all payment obligations on your property are covered by your rental income. Essentially, your tenants are paying down your mortgage for you.

After expenses, the initial cash flow from each individual property may seem minimal. But across a larger, growing portfolio, your monthly cash flow becomes much more substantial. If you also plan carefully, with a long-term investment strategy, you will eventually have properties with no debt service and a steady stream of passive income. This allows you to create long-term, intergenerational wealth for your family; for more information, see Chapter Nine.

**Direct Control Over Your Investment**

We believe that income-producing properties are the best types of investment; as a tangible or hard asset, real estate offers more control than other types of investments. For example, a mutual fund portfolio will move with the stock market; any rumors or investor speculation can create wild fluctuations in how it performs. You can sell or buy more, but

in terms of controlling its value there is not much you can do except watch your investment go up and down. With real estate, however, there are many factors under your direct control.

For properties that are being bought, held, and rented out, you can control whether or not to make improvements to increase the rental rate you desire. This ability to physically influence your asset offers tremendous opportunities to improve its value (this is discussed further in Chapter Six). You can also be proactive and creative in your marketing to attract quality tenants and increase your rental income.

Although the real estate market moves slowly, this can work to your benefit. As long as you do your homework before investing, you can ride out any down cycles. A well-managed rental property, in which you are keeping your vacancy rate low, will continue to generate income during an economic downturn as you invest in the reduced-price properties available at that time. Read Chapter Four for more information.

Finally, as with other investments, you can choose to sell your property when you feel the time is right. Investing in real estate offers considerable diversity to your portfolio, providing another level of control; Chapter Three explores this topic in greater detail.

## How Leslie Left the "Rat Race"

I'm not sure exactly when I realized that real estate investing was my passion. As a child growing up, I watched my parents acquire and manage a small portfolio of townhomes in partnership with our neighbors and friends, the Patel family. For a while, they self-managed these properties until they came to their senses and hired a qualified property manager.

As children—me, my brother, and the Patel's children, Seema and Rajiv—we were recruited to help clean and paint the units

before new tenants arrived. For the most part, we had a great time being involved and getting our hands dirty. It was exciting to watch the transformation of a property through our work. And I got a rush from finding the hidden gems (in other words, junk) that tenants had left behind. The reward for all our youthful enthusiasm and help was usually a pizza dinner.

I was too young to understand why owning these properties was a good idea, but I had a great time. Like many children, my brother and I had visions of becoming astronauts, firefighters, policemen, archaeologists, or other interesting occupations. But not once did I think about becoming a full-time real estate investor. My parents took the time to instill a good work ethic in us, but we thought that we were supposed to finish school and get a good job, or settle into a reputable profession, as they had.

While in university, I always had part-time jobs but basically didn't know what I wanted to do. I found it odd that we were supposed to choose our career when many of us were still uncertain about what we loved to do. But I followed the herd, chose a major, graduated, and began working. Eventually, I got married and had my son, Ethan.

I am an advocate of lifelong education, always taking a part-time course or reading different kinds of books. Eventually, I picked up the book *Rich Dad Poor Dad* by Robert T. Kiyosaki and Sharon L. Lechter . If I could identify a turning point in my life, it would probably be reading that book. It helped me to see things in a whole new light. I realized that, to create the wealth and abundance I desired in my life, I would have to take a different path than the rest of the herd.

Kiyosaki talks about being caught up in the 'rat race' and I realized how true this was. For many of us, instead of changing how we did things, we stayed with what was comfortable and ran around in circles, day after day, like a hamster on a spinning wheel. I used to commute by train and the symbolism was quite ironic.

Thousands of us would park our cars at the station, cram into a train packed as tight as a can of sardines, ride downtown in a daze, then walk through the city's underground plazas like zombies, heading straight for the buildings that caged all of us during the long workday. I never deviated from my regular path; I even stopped at the same coffee shop at the same time every single morning. After putting in a long day, I would take the same path back home.

I was like a rat in a familiar maze. The problem was that there would be no cheese at the end of my maze. In my career, I experienced the frustration of putting in endless hours and effort to be rewarded with a paltry 3% raise; this was my company's maximum allowed reward for busting my chops all year. At the time it worked out to an extra $75 a month, before taxes, and wasn't much of an incentive. I began to look at our financial situation and realized that, if we did not make any changes in our lives, we would forever be dependent on the whims of an indifferent employer.

After an inventory of our assets and liabilities, and taking inflation into account, I also realized that our minimal savings would not be enough to support our desired lifestyle well into retirement. We needed to do something dramatic. I had big goals and dreams and realized that, if I was ever going to accomplish them and enjoy my life fully, I would have to get out of my comfort zone and stop working for someone else.

At the same time, I realized how much value we had in our home. We had purchased a brand new, three-bedroom home in an excellent subdivision in Burlington, Ontario. Although we had lived there for only three years, we had watched its value grow; this was during a time when the market was escalating rapidly. We had originally purchased our home for approximately $195,000. When the time came to sell we listed it for $274,900 and received a conditional offer within two days. After some negotiation, we sold our property for $274,000. It brought back memories of my parents' townhome portfolio, and it wasn't long before we decided to purchase our first investment property.

Today, I have expanded my portfolio to include commercial real estate and am focused on providing solid, profitable investment opportunities to my corporate investors in that market. I've been investing for several years now, but am still as passionate and excited as when I first got started. I know many people say that real estate is supposed to be boring. Maybe the actual analysis and transactions are, but the thrill of building and managing my business and my portfolio keeps me up all night and gets me jumping out of bed in the morning.

I'm completely happy with my life and the fact that I am actively taking control of my destiny. As I continue to grow my own real estate investment business, I remember to surround myself with others who share my mindset. All this positive energy provides me with the strength and focus I need to overcome the many challenges along the way.

# Chapter Two

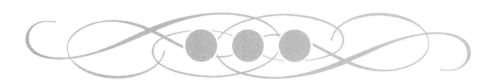

## *Winning Strategies:*

### DEVELOPING THE MINDSET OF SUCCESS

To achieve the most profit from our proprietary strategy for real estate investing, you must develop the mindset of a wealthy, successful investor. Our experience indicates that this mindset is essential. Its two keys are a positive, optimistic perspective and an entrepreneurial outlook. Together, these powerful attitudes will help you to develop other important traits, including determination, perseverance, the ability to effectively set and achieve goals, and resistance to fear. The sum of all these qualities is an outstanding ability to take action and overcome all obstacles to creating wealth through real estate investing.

### Expect Success

There is no question that we live in a land of opportunity. There are many ways to succeed in life, financially and personally, and with the mindset of success there are no limits to what you can achieve. In matters of wealth, happiness, healthy relationships, and ambitions, you don't have to know in advance how you're going to accomplish your goals and dreams. But you must believe that you will. To achieve success, it is vital that you first expect to succeed.

A small percentage of the world's population earns more than 90% of all the money. This is not necessarily because they are better or smarter than you. It's because they have developed a positive, optimistic attitude that puts them in a prime position for success.

Positive-minded people don't seem to be any more intelligent than negative-minded people. They don't have a particular advantage in life and their social status doesn't seem to be a factor. But they are perceptive; they will recognize great opportunities with the potential for success, and they have the confidence to turn those opportunities into stunning triumphs.

We all have tremendous potential for achievement, but are held back by self-doubt and a lack of self-confidence. There are ways to overcome this, and it is crucial that you do. You cannot expect other people to respect you, or your goals, if you don't.

All people have the ability to succeed by developing a positive attitude, but not all choose to think this way. If asked, most people wouldn't identify themselves as negative minded. They will claim they have a positive attitude, and then give dozens of reasons why they can't achieve their goals in life. Most people live with a negative frame of mind, content to work their nine-to-five job, year after year, paycheck to paycheck, for the rest of their lives because of fear. They fear they can't do better, or they fear failure.

## Overcoming Fear

*Fear of failure.* We all have doubts, such as, "I'm not good enough to succeed at the goals I have set, or smart enough to handle any crises that may arise along the way." If we let them, our doubts can paralyze us from even trying, they can cheat us of the joy in achieving our goals, and they can prevent us from achieving financial or personal success.

If you believe that you will fail, then you have set yourself up for failure. If you live your life, day to day, focusing on the things you don't want to happen in your life, such as the fear of failure, then you will have a life filled will negative things and a long list of failures. You will create a negative mindset and will get exactly what you expect.

You need to focus on what you want. Then your mind will begin programming itself for success. Be clear about what you desire the most. What goals do you want to achieve?

With a positive mindset, visualize your goals in your mind and "see" yourself successfully achieving them. Do not visualize how you're going to get there, but only that you are going to get there. Feel the positive emotions that will come along with your success. You are telling your mind that you will achieve these things and it will respond to what you want. Here are some techniques for strengthening goals within your mind.

1. Write down your goals and describe them in detail. Then read them over and over again. The key to success is believing that you will achieve what you wrote.

2. Cut out pictures of the things you desire and the goals you want to achieve. Create a visual representation of your goals and desires—this is commonly called a "vision board." Place this vision board where you will see it most often to remind yourself about what goals you have set to achieve and keep your mindset positive.

By focusing only on the successes in your life, you will learn to manage the fear of failure. You will learn to achieve your goals in life, and feel the satisfaction that comes from each success, which will continue to drive you. Successful people fail all the time but they look for the lesson within each failure; then they get up and try again. They also push themselves past the fear by focusing their energy on how it will feel when they accomplish their new goals.

*Fear of losing money.* You will never meet a rich person who has not lost money at some point in their life. Everyone has the fear of losing money, but rich, successful people will not allow fear or doubt to control their thoughts and emotions or diminish their positive mindset. Failure inspires these winners to achieve more. This is the secret to their success: how they handle fear.

A less successful person will allow fear and doubt to overpower his or her thoughts and create a negative mindset; this is a formula for failure. With most people, the fear of losing money is greater than the joy of becoming rich. The main reason that more than 90% of people struggle financially is that they play it safe and never take risks to realize their dream of becoming wealthy. These people will also never experience the joy in success and achievement.

To overcome fear, we must step out of our comfort zone and take risks. In the field of creating wealth, bankers and financial planners are often viewed as confident, positive-thinking people, but this is not always the case. They are adept at offering suggestions for investing your money, not theirs. This creates no fear or negative thoughts of failure because there is no risk to them or their personal wealth if your investments don't do well. When it comes time for these financial experts to invest their own money, however, their true mindsets are revealed.

Financial professionals are just as vulnerable to fear, doubt, and negative thinking. If they haven't developed effective ways to counter this negative mindset, they may not invest at

32

all, even if it is the same investment they recommended to you. A banker may handle money daily but this does not guarantee wealth or success unless his or her interest in finance is accompanied by a positive mindset.

*Fear of not being good enough.* Always remember that people with a positive mindset expect to succeed, but people with a negative mindset expect to fail. They often blame their lack of confidence on external influences.

For example, some people believe that their lack of education is holding them back, and yet there are many people with college or university degrees who lack what it takes to succeed. In today's world, a person may finish school at the top of his or her class but fail to do well when applying that knowledge outside the classroom. We have all seen people with college or university degrees working at fast food restaurants or other low-paying jobs.

Success is not always determined by the grades that students get in school; their attitude is another big factor. Teachers have reported that, when asking a question in class, many students will not offer an answer for fear of giving the wrong one, while other students will quickly raise their hands. The latter students are positive thinkers: they will not fear trying, and will feel joy and satisfaction when their answer is correct.

The students who won't even try are lacking self-confidence and courage—in short, the mindset to achieve their goals. Negative thinking, self-doubt, and the fear of failure will severely hamper their future.

One student may have a higher grade average than another student, but if the one with lower grades also possesses a positive mindset and the courage to overcome fear, he or she is more likely to succeed in the real world. This is one reason why teachers encourage students to set aside their fears and take risks when answering questions or solving problems. It helps to eliminate the fear of failure, increases their self-confidence, and puts them in a more positive frame of mind. This increases their chances for success.

To succeed in the real world, it is as important to develop self-confidence and a positive mindset as it is to get good grades in school.

### Rick's Friend Gets Stopped by Fear

Many people desire to be real estate investors but, even after many courses and seminars, never invest simply out of fear. Years ago, when I was just getting started in real estate investing, I shared my venture with a childhood classmate. He was a close friend and quickly became interested in how I went about obtaining properties. After months of learning and watching what I was accomplishing in the real estate market, he asked me to help him get started with his first investment.

All people have the ability to succeed with a positive mindset, but my friend let fear affect his desire and ability to succeed. I researched some excellent investment opportunities for him, all with a positive cash flow and in areas with plans for future development. But even after completing the due diligence measures that are essential to success, and proving to him that these were good solid investments, he was still too nervous to invest.

He was only willing to invest in real estate if I would agree to go in on the investment with him. His fear of investing on his own was too great. He believed that a joint venture would ensure the success of his real estate investment. I spent time explaining the importance of doing proper research, including how to do an area study and property analysis. Despite spending months educating my friend on real estate and real estate investing, his fear was too great to invest on his own.

More than ten years have passed and, to this day, my friend continues to let the fear of failure control him. His fear has prevented him from investing in any type of real estate property. Many people would rather play it safe out of the fear of failure than enjoy all the success they could achieve in their life with a positive mindset.

## Leslie's Entrepreneurial Outlook

As I said in Chapter One, the road to true wealth requires leaving the "rat race" and becoming your own employer. It took a while for me to figure this out, but the journey was worth it. My father taught me that an entrepreneurial outlook is an important element in the mindset of success.

After graduating from university, I spent a few years working for a mutual fund company, first as a sales assistant and eventually as a junior analyst in the finance department. All the while my father encouraged me to join the family business. He went out of his way to emphasize that, to create true wealth, one had to have an entrepreneurial outlook. But I was stubborn and fixated on making it on my own.

After being in an academic environment for so many years, it seemed natural to enter the workforce and begin climbing the corporate ladder, just like my father did—at first. But after being passed up for a promotion (which at the time seemed like a negative event), my father left Ontario Hydro to start a business with several of his colleagues. This not only meant leaving a stable and solid income stream, it also meant nurturing and growing new skills as an entrepreneur.

Having a particular skill doesn't necessarily make someone a good business owner. My father has a Ph.D., but things were not easy during the early years of starting his company. His academic skills and engineering expertise helped him develop a service that was in demand. But he had to deal with long hours, unexpected obstacles, inexperience in running a business, and many other challenges.

Rather than giving up and going back to a corporate job, my father persevered and continued to move forward. It took almost five years and many sacrifices before he began to see the fruits of his labor. Even after things started to take off, he faced challenge after challenge, and yet my father never gave up.

This is why attitude is important. How you interpret the events in your life and use them to motivate you to persevere and overcome obstacles is integral to developing the mindset of success.

Eventually, I came to my senses and joined my dad in the family business for about ten years before launching my real estate investment company. During that time, I learned how to think like an entrepreneur and experienced the trials and tribulations of running your own business.

Some people see it as an escape from the rat race and a great way to live life by doing something they love. But they often forget that running a business is just that: learning the mechanics of being successful as their own boss. They get caught up in fantasies of making a lot of money instead of focusing on important factors such as knowing how to be of service to others and the value they can offer to clients.

To this day, as our business grows, we come across newer and bigger challenges but this is part of success. Although I no longer work in my father's firm on a day-to-day basis, I still have partial oversight over the finances and am also on the advisory board. We believe in the company and our ability to run it well. With each challenge, we take the time to understand the underlying lesson while never ceasing to push forward.

Most people look at a well-run company and assume that you are lucky, but believe me it's not luck that got my father to where he is today. I have been fortunate to witness it firsthand and learn the lessons he shares in his role as my greatest mentor.

### Defying the Cynics

When you develop a positive mindset, you attract the same kind of people into your life. Surrounding yourself with such people helps you to stay positive and focused on the goals you want to achieve. But the same goes for very negative people; with their dark outlook and mindset about life, they will attract and surround themselves with similar types of negative people. The world is full of such people, and they all want to bring you down to their level.

They will try to sidetrack your dreams of success, declaring that you will fail to achieve your goals. They will say that you are crazy for taking such risks. Friends or family may say things such as, "What makes you think you can do that?" or "That will never work." If you allow it to happen, they will plant such seeds of doubt and fear in your mind that you will end up thinking they are right. Then you may fail to act and stay with what's safe while opportunities pass you by.

The world is full of doubters predicting doom and gloom. They will never become financially or personally successful in their lives. They are filled with fear, focus only on the negative, and never play to win. Under their influence, you will never get the chance to accomplish your goals.

It takes a great deal of courage to rise above the doubters that you will encounter along your path to success. But remember that most people are prevented from becoming wealthy because they allow themselves be influenced by negativity.

The main thing that keeps people poor is that they criticize instead of analyze. Someone who criticizes, does not analyze, or allows doubts and fears to close his or her mind is a cynic. To succeed, you must learn to overcome cynicism. As a positive-thinking person, you must develop strategies for dealing with the negativity that you will constantly encounter. This will accelerate your success.

Combat the negative talk of doom and gloom with a positive mindset. Conquer the fears and doubts that could derail the goals you are trying to achieve. Stand firm on good, solid research as your standard for action, not rumors and cynicism.

A negative mindset leads to negative emotions such as anger, depression, and resentment. People who embrace these negative emotions will never be poised for success. But those with a positive mindset know the passion of working to achieve their goals and the joy and satisfaction as they experience success.

There are many advantages to having a positive outlook toward life. In addition to greater wealth and success, they include the finer emotions such as joy, passion, and satisfaction.

### Rick's Positive Inspiration

I have always had a positive mindset for success. It began with the optimism that was part of my close-knit family. But it was strengthened after seeing my mother, at the age of 38, go back to school and achieve her goal of becoming a financial consultant.

My mother was hired as a financial advisor for a well-established financial institution. She possessed a mindset for success and continued to achieve better positions with higher pay in the company of her choice. She was a huge influence in my life. She showed me that you can accomplish any goal you desire if you have the right mindset.

During her fight against lung cancer, despite the great deal of pain she endured, there was not a day that went by in which she didn't say how proud she was of what I had accomplished. My mother was my biggest supporter and inspiration in my life. She believed in me and claimed I would be successful at accomplishing anything I set my mind to.

On December 25, 2008, with me by her side, my mother lost her fight with cancer. It was the hardest day of my life, but I feel that she is still with me, guiding me as I continue to make her proud. Her ability to overcome major obstacles and achieve success in her life empowers me to succeed. She

proved that, despite coming from a poor family, you can achieve anything you desire.

There are no limits if you possess the right mindset. I will never forget the lessons she taught me.

### The Cure for Laziness

Laziness is another potential roadblock to your financial or personal success. Busy people are often the laziest; they keep busy, working long hours or more than one job, just to avoid the hard work of changing what they do and the way they think. Many people believe that the only way to get ahead in life is to work as hard as they can, save as much money as they can, and spend as little as possible.

A lazy mind accepts that they can't succeed or do better in life. Perhaps failure has made your spirit angry and your lazy mind must find excuses to justify why you can't succeed. For example, you may think, "It's too much bother" or "It's not safe, I might lose money." What is the cure for laziness? A little greed—with a positive approach, greed is not a bad thing.

We all have a level of greed in us, such as wanting more from life: a nice house, a sports car, a big boat, or the ability to travel. Anyone can work three jobs to create the wealth they desire, but does this allow them to create joy and happiness at the same time? In their extreme effort to acquire wealth, they are not left with any time to enjoy life and often become bitter.

Many people would rather play it safe in life out of the fear of failure than enjoy the success they could acquire by developing a positive mindset. Let your greed, or desire for the good things in life, motivate you to succeed. Set your mind to what you want to have and from that you will attract a clear desire to achieve it.

If you see it in your mind, you will achieve what you desire. Stay focused on what you are trying to accomplish and believe

in your ability to achieve it. By doing so, you will attain the inner strength and peace of mind necessary to overcome the obstacles you will face. Once you have that focus, get out there and take action every day.

**Rick Learns to Create Wealth**

Wealth can be described in many ways. What does it mean to you? Is it possible for the average person to become wealthy? Is financial wealth about having enough money to retire at the age of 65, or perhaps affording the home of your dreams? And is it ever too late to start on the road to financial security? I believe that, whatever constitutes your definition of wealth, you can achieve it with the right mindset.

I came from a family where my parents struggled financially, even though my father worked eight hours a day, forty hours a week. I saw, even as a young child, the effect it had on my parents when they could not afford to provide us with the same things as other kids.

At the age of eleven, I worked in a farmer's field, picking tomatoes and other vegetables seven days a week during the summer holidays while my friends played sports or went on family vacations. This was the only way I could get the money to buy the things other kids had.

It was a tough life for my family financially but it brought us closer together. My parents always provided us with support and a loving home and did the best they could with what they had for me and my three brothers. But I was determined, even at a young age, to achieve more in life than struggling from paycheck to paycheck.

Before I started a career as a real estate investor, I worked for years in product distribution. I always desired to enter the world of real estate investing but was secure in my job and was not in the right mindset at the time. It wasn't until I was faced with closure of the distribution facility where I worked that I decided to follow my passion.

Up to this point, I had only a basic understanding of investing in real estate but, with a positive attitude, I educated myself through books, seminars, and networking with many experienced and successful entrepreneurs. I would often be doing research on my computer until the early hours of the morning to obtain more knowledge. I quickly learned that education brought with it increased confidence. It helped me to develop a positive mindset of success that I needed to create wealth through real estate investing.

I believe the keys to wealth are education, having a positive mindset, and support from family and friends. I have followed these steps to create and manage a well-diversified real estate portfolio, as well as a successful stock market portfolio.

### Leslie's Family Mindset

Creating wealth is about more than the accumulation of material goods. It is about a sense of fulfillment, and living the life of your dreams—today, and not as some far-off, distant vision. It is about the power to control your own destiny: understanding that it lies in your hands and does not depend on any past circumstances.

I'm fascinated by how so many self-made millionaires and billionaires were able to defeat the odds and achieve such great success. Many of them share their stories of humble beginnings and underprivileged lives. Whether it was family turmoil, financial instability, or some other seemingly insurmountable challenge, they managed to move forward and achieve unbelievable success. By reading many of their stories, I came to realize that the ability to achieve great success must come from within.

Inside each one of us is the ability to create an energetic life of passion, abundance, and happiness. I truly believe that, no matter where we are today or where we come from, we are all capable of so much more. The story of my own upbringing, compared to that of my parents, is like Charles Dickens' *A Tale of Two Cities*. From two completely different backgrounds—one of poverty and one of privilege—we managed to achieve success because we have a positive, success-oriented, and entrepreneurial mindset.

I come from a very loving, nurturing, and supportive family. My parents gave my brother and I everything we needed while we were growing up, not just in material goods but in terms of teaching us valuable life lessons. Without their support and example, I would not be where I am today. I am fortunate to have grown up very privileged.

In my middle-income neighborhood, we had food, clothing, shelter, toys, vacations, and a well-rounded education. My story may seem a little boring compared to the struggles faced by other wealthy individuals. Some may suggest that my current success is the result of living a privileged life, and that my journey toward the fulfillment of my goals and dreams must be easier because of my past. They may say how lucky I was to have been given so much.

They may say that, if they had been given the same upbringing, they would also achieve the success that I currently enjoy. I am grateful for all the things I am fortunate to have been given. But I want to tell them: grow up and stop making excuses for where you are today! The only person stopping you from living your dreams today is you and your limiting beliefs.

All of us, regardless of our past, have the ability to be truly wealthy in all areas of our lives. Many individuals whose upbringings were similar to mine are struggling to make ends meet. And there are people who have had more difficult lives that are more successful than I am.

If upbringing and environment were the only factors in financial success, then the friends I grew up with—who enjoyed the same things I had—should be living the life of their dreams today. But many of them aren't. To achieve

phenomenal success, you must possess a winning and success-oriented mindset. You must believe in yourself and your ability to reach the milestones you set.

My parents grew up in a very different, much poorer environment and, in comparison, have achieved much greater success than I have. There is a much wider gap between where they came from and where they are today, and they faced many more obstacles and challenges.

They grew up in the Philippines with only the bare necessities. My dad tells stories of how, as a child, he rose early each morning to sell fresh bread to bring money home. The fancy toys I enjoyed as a child were, for him, just a fantasy. He and his friends made their own toys with whatever odds and ends they could find. My dad learned to appreciate little things like the pleasure of jumping in puddles during a rainstorm. To this day, he still reminisces about his childhood and the exhilaration of enjoying the rain. It's funny how, when you have so little, you seem to have a better sense of appreciation for everything around you.

During visits to the Philippines, I was humbled to see where my parents grew up and how different it was from my Canadian upbringing. The things I have always taken for granted suddenly seemed like such luxuries. Young children in the village were intrigued by the toiletries, books, and toys I had in my backpack. I remember sitting on the porch with my grandparents, in the extreme heat (with no air conditioning), wondering what it was like for my parents to grow up there. I am amazed at how much effort it took for them to achieve all the success they enjoy!

Both my parents left the Philippines in their late teens. My father joined the U.S. Navy and tells many stories about the obstacles he overcame while he served in the military. After finishing nursing school in the Philippines, my mother came to the U.S. to work as a nurse. She also had her share of trials adjusting to this new environment.

They eventually moved to Canada and got married, and my mother worked long hours as a nurse while my father studied. Eventually, he received a Ph.D. in nuclear physics at McMaster University. They sacrificed financially, and in the time they spent together, but they got through it and eventually started a family. I was born in 1972 and my brother arrived four years later.

Growing up, our lives were pretty average from a Canadian perspective but starkly different from a Philippines perspective. My mother continued to work part time as a nurse and my father spent 25 years working at Ontario Hydro. The series of events that caused him to leave that job allowed our family to build a successful and profitable business called Advanced Measurement and Analysis Group Inc.

My point is this: there is absolutely no reason why we can't live the life of our dreams today. My parents, with their background of privation, immigrated to North America with not much more than the shirts on their backs. They created an extraordinary amount of wealth and success; with my privileged upbringing, I should be able to achieve as much and more. I'm not saying that it's a simple process but it begins with a mindset of success. Start by developing that mindset, and then consistently taking action, and you'll be on your way to creating true wealth.

Many have taken for granted the abundant environment we are fortunate to live in. Some have stories similar to mine; their parents had very little but provided well for their families and grew their wealth. Others, with stories similar to Rick's, grew up struggling financially. What differentiates the winners from the losers is what you have learned from your life experiences and how you move forward to create abundance and wealth in all areas of your life.

# Chapter Three

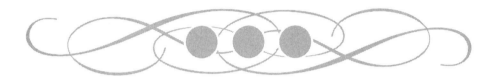

## *Sky Scraping:*

### BUILDING A PORTFOLIO FOR MAXIMUM SUCCESS

*"The loftier the building, the deeper must the foundation be laid."*
— Thomas Kempis

Building a successful real estate portfolio is comparable to a contractor's process of planning, building, and finishing a quality investment property. In this chapter, this analogy will help to illustrate how you can ensure maximum success from your future investments.

All profitable construction projects follow a clearly defined series of steps, or actions that must be taken, to ensure success. The final product will differ but the process is essentially the same. Building a real estate portfolio follows a similar step-by-step progression.

## Step 1: Plan for a Solid Foundation

Engineers know that, for any building to last, the most critical element is a well-planned foundation. When engineering your real estate portfolio, apply the same philosophy; do the necessary groundwork to ensure that your portfolio will stand the test of time.

Good planning, which is central to the success of any worthwhile project, will lay a firm foundation for your portfolio. Take the time to clearly define your vision for investing in real estate; this will form the basis for all your future efforts. Put pen to paper and write it out: your dreams for the future; the kind of property you want to own; and how you plan to interact with the properties you acquire. Then plot that vision into a timeline, with concrete goals that reflect what you expect to achieve by investing in real estate.

The journey toward success is often long and riddled with obstacles, so build your foundation deep to withstand any stress. The key lies in a well-anchored understanding of what you are trying to accomplish. Do you want passive income to support your present or future lifestyle so that you can do the things you enjoy? Or are you looking to build a solid net worth while continuing to work in your current career?

You need to be clear about the results you want to see, and why. Then your actions will align with your vision and your investment strategies will be tied into your long-term goals.

## Step 2: Begin Construction

Now you can confidently begin construction on your real estate portfolio, using the foundation you created to enhance your success. Every construction site is bustling with plenty of activity, which is the key to this stage: taking action.

Successful people are always in motion, trying new things, taking the next step, and seeing what works. This doesn't

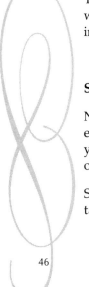

mean they don't make mistakes. But they are committed to learning whatever they can from each mistake, and then getting up and moving forward again. Rely on your foundation of understanding why you are investing, and then take positive action.

Many people spend their time learning about real estate investing; success comes from working with that knowledge. All real estate investors need to increase their knowledge by reading books, taking courses, browsing through the specifications of various properties, and so forth. But for some, the fear of taking that important step—of acquiring their first property—prevents them from moving forward.

To become a successful real estate investor, you must be action-oriented: try something new, be open to making mistakes as a part of learning, and work through any fear you may experience rather than becoming paralyzed by it. Success doesn't happen overnight…but success won't happen at all unless you take action.

### Step 3: Support the Structure

Unlike the rigid structure of a fixed building, your growing portfolio will need something more flexible to accommodate new opportunities while building yourself for success. Your confidence will be boosted by developing different tools that you will need to succeed. Investing in these skills will enable you to make solid, effective decisions, resulting in good structural support for your goals.

Start by learning the lingo. Every industry has its own language and real estate investing is no different. A good working knowledge of commonly used terms will increase your confidence about communicating with your support team as well as potential joint-venture partners and clients. It also helps to avoid misunderstandings by ensuring that everyone is working with the same frame of reference.

Along with these fundamentals, you must also become an expert at the process of investing in real estate. These are the tools of your trade: analyzing profitable investment opportunities; examining financial issues such as positive cash flow, loans, leveraging, and joint ventures; understanding the steps involved in negotiating an offer; transferring ownership, including paying land transfer and other taxes; and preparing for the closing. And that's just what happens during a sale, not to mention becoming a landlord and effectively managing your properties.

After identifying a favorable opportunity, you must also polish your sales skills. They'll come into play when persuading joint-venture partners or clients of the value you are providing with a prospective investment. This will include taking the time to listen and understand people's needs, which is another skill that you must strengthen.

In this step, the key to your success is also your greatest asset: your knowledge and ability to work creatively with others. Take the time to ensure that your framework is firm. Credibility and respect come from showing that you not only talk the talk but understand it fully and practice what you preach.

**Step 4: Call in the Trades**

You have your own strengths. Complement them with solidly built, mutually beneficial relationships. In the same way that a building's completion depends on the work of many different trades, focus on what you are good at and delegate the rest to other experts. As we will discuss in Chapter Eight, surround yourself with a strong success team of professionals, including realtors, appraisers, lenders, lawyers, and accountants. Your investment projects will benefit from their expertise.

Do the same with potential joint-venture partners. By continually expanding your network, you will ensure greater access to prospective opportunities and financing partners. We all have financial limits; expand your resource base by teaming up with others. This will help you to grow your portfolio much more quickly.

Each trade has its own expertise, and yours is creating more wealth. Learning to delegate is very important to your success. In an effort to save money, many new investors try to do everything themselves. This can work for a small portfolio, but it is unrealistic if you wish to grow yours. Remaining focused on the countless tasks of acquiring and managing each property won't allow you the freedom to seek out and analyze profitable new investments.

Keep in mind the role you play on your team and the skills you are perfecting. Ensure that you spend your time increasing your wealth as an educated, savvy investor. By carefully selecting a team of experts to complement your skills, you can grow your portfolio that much faster.

**Step 5: Finishing Touches**

Once your portfolio begins to grow, take the time to ensure that you run it as an efficient, valuable business. A building's worth increases with the quality of its finishing touches, and your portfolio will similarly benefit from attending to the important details.

Put your creativity into gear by devising innovative marketing to attract quality tenants. Although it may take some time and ingenuity, it will pay off in the long run. It can often save you a lot of money and reduces the hassle of troublesome or disrespectful tenants.

Keeping your properties well maintained will help to attract quality tenants. Ensure that your properties reflect a sense of pride that they can share. In addition, be responsive to the needs of your tenants. After all, they are your clients. They are making payments to you that are paying down your

mortgage. Provide them with quality customer service and build a mutually respectful relationship for minimum hassles and maximum profit.

Finding additional ways to generate income is another essential detail. Read books and newspapers, network with other real estate investors, and open your mind to new ideas that can potentially increase your revenue. Different sources of information will help you to identify novel ways to improve each property's profit potential. One effective tactic involves implementing an improvement program to position a property for the highest and best use; top-quality rental properties generate the highest returns.

Hiring experienced property management to oversee the daily details will free your mind from worry and liberate your talents. Develop a good working relationship, set clear expectations for the standards to which your property must be maintained, and then leave your managers to it and get busy acquiring new investments. Even if you own one property, hiring management is worth considering; the cost is offset by the time savings, which will enable you to create more wealth through real estate investment.

### Leveraging Helps Build Your Portfolio Faster

Donald Trump is passionate about real estate. "It's tangible, it's solid, it's beautiful. It's artistic, from my standpoint, and I just love real estate." In addition to the aesthetic beauty of ventures such as Trump Towers in New York City, tremendous financial savvy helps get the greatest worth out of his projects. Experienced investors such as Trump know that real estate's value as a tangible, or hard, asset means that financing for this kind of investment is readily available. Leveraging makes the most use of it.

"Leverage is the art of using other people's resources to reach your goals," writes Michael Sexton, president, on the Trump

University Web site. Leveraging is one of the main benefits of investing in real estate because it helps to maximize your ability to build your portfolio. The key to your success is utilizing leverage wisely while understanding the other factors that will affect your real estate investment portfolio.

Globefund.com defines leverage as "The financial advantage of an investment that controls property of greater value than the cash invested. Leverage is usually achieved through the use of borrowed money." Significant wealth can be built with investment real estate through this kind of borrowing. It stretches your financial resources. You utilize the power of leverage by borrowing the bulk of the funds to acquire a property. The bank lends this money in return for interest; the amount of cash you need to contribute is usually only 25% and even less with an insured mortgage.

This is what we call "good debt" because it is incurred to acquire an income-generating asset, which grows in value year after year in the form of appreciation. Many people perceive all debt to be bad and undesirable. It is the financially successful investor who understands the difference between good debt and bad debt. Here's a simple definition: "When you buy something that goes down in value immediately, that's bad debt," says David Bach, CEO of Finish Rich Inc. and author of *The Finish Rich Workbook*.

An example of bad debt would be purchasing a car using a loan. A car is a depreciating asset that goes down in value, year after year, and you will never increase the value of this investment. But good debt is "investment debt that creates value; for example, student loans, real estate loans, home mortgages, and business loans," says Eric Gelb, CEO of Gateway Financial Advisors and author of *Getting Started in Asset Allocation*.

Taking out a mortgage to acquire an investment property is an example of good debt, but only if you follow the correct steps. Provided that you did your due diligence before making the purchase, and then manage the property effectively, you can expect it to increase in value over time. (Read Rick's story about due diligence at the end of this chapter; property management is discussed in Chapter Eight.)

In addition, a well-managed investment property, located in an area poised for future growth, can bring in monthly income. But keep in mind that there is a delicate balance between leverage and cash flow. Generally speaking, the more leveraged your investment property, the less cash flow you will receive. With a more leveraged investment, your monthly payments are higher. (Since the real estate market is cyclical, it is important to ensure that you can carry the higher payments consistent with a larger debt load if your property goes vacant. See Chapter Five for more information about positive cash flow.)

The following examples illustrate why investing in the tangible asset of real estate is considered good debt, and how the power of leverage helps you to profit the most from that debt.

### Rick Describes Beginner Mistakes to Avoid

One of the biggest mistakes that you, as an investor, can make is not taking the time to become well educated in the field of real estate investing before making your first purchase. Educating yourself is the key to success and a good working knowledge of the business is essential. I spent a great deal of time attending real estate courses and seminars, reading books, doing online research, and attending related networking events before I bought my first property.

Many first-time investors will jump into their first real estate investment without properly understanding how to succeed with their venture. Most beginners tend to follow the herd, imitating what other investors are doing, and they assume it is the right way. But this is extremely unwise, and the outcome will often be costly.

Never make assumptions about any aspect of a prospective real estate investment. Be sure to fully understand the market before making a purchase. Invest plenty of time in a thorough analysis. Relying on proper research can make the difference between a successful and unsuccessful real estate investment.

A few years ago, I was approached by a close friend with an offer to purchase his home. He explained that he would sell his house to me for $30,000 below the price that he could get by using a realtor. This sounded like a great deal and an excellent investment opportunity. But after researching this property, I discovered the house was valued at $20,000 below the great deal that was being offered by my close friends. If I had assumed it was a profitable deal, based on what I was being told, I would have overpaid by $20,000 on this investment.

Do not buy any real estate property without comparing similar properties that were recently sold in the surrounding area. You risk paying more than the property is worth. Overpaying for a property can greatly affect the return on your investment.

In addition, be sure to ask a lot of questions and listen to the professionals with knowledge about your potential investment. If you build a solid team of proven experts who are willing to give you advice, you can significantly enhance your success in every deal (see Chapter Seven).

You must consult both real estate and financing professionals. Talk to your real estate agent and a qualified appraiser; and also consult with lawyers, accountants, and bankers to get different perspectives about your prospect. Other resources for information are landlords, tenants, the local municipal planning department, and anyone else you can think of. Be sure to learn as much as possible about the property and the area prior to investing.

Your due diligence about a potential real estate investment means that you also need to do a complete, formal area study.

This includes evaluating the infrastructure, vacancy rates, and future development plans in and around the area (for more information, see Chapter Five). Give yourself enough time to do this necessary research before making your decision.

I have seen many properties that looked good on paper. But my due diligence research revealed that they were located in an area with high vacancy rates, or with poor infrastructure where the city did not have plans for development. At first glance, a property may look like an excellent investment opportunity, but allowing myself time to complete the due diligence demonstrated that it was not a solid or profitable investment. I have walked away from many such deals.

Three of the best ways to make money in real estate are cash flow, appreciation, and equity growth through mortgage pay-down. Because I'm looking for a solid real estate investment, I always complete my due diligence with these top three methods of growth in mind.

# Chapter Four

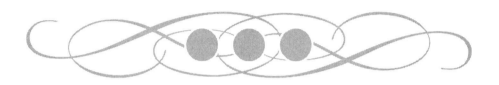

## *Creating Wealth:*

### THE FACTS ABOUT FINANCIAL LITERACY

We believe that financial literacy is vitally important because it contributes to the mindset you need to develop to be a successful investor. It includes your attitude about becoming wealthy and your ability to utilize financial information to create wealth by investing in real estate. Unfortunately, most academic instruction does not cover wealth creation or financial literacy, which has doomed many seemingly successful people with prestigious careers to a lifetime of living paycheck to paycheck.

For such people, their lifestyle tends to grow with their annual pay increase or bonus, but that's where it stops. They do not have the knowledge required to make their money start working for them, and are unable to put in place a financial team to help. They have to work until retirement and hope that there's enough money to maintain their expected lifestyle throughout their golden years.

Although this is acceptable for most of the population, you are reading this book because you do not accept it! You picked up this book because you want to get out of the rat race described by Robert Kiyosaki in Chapter One. And a good grasp of the fundamentals of financial literacy and wealth creation is an important contributor to your success.

At the end of the day, people who are still in that rat race may feel they have security and stability. But their livelihood is at the mercy of company management. Their future can be drastically affected by an economy where seemingly stable companies suddenly dissolve. People can find themselves suddenly unemployed and unable to maintain their lifestyle while searching for new employment.

The truly successful are never satisfied with the status quo of corporate security and stability; they continually push to take on the next challenge. They are people of action, willing to do whatever it takes to reach their personal financial goals. We are not suggesting there is anything wrong with being career-oriented or focused on moving up in your company. But it is equally important to build your personal asset base, thereby putting yourself in a strong economic position. Then you can support your lifestyle regardless of what happens in the nine-to-five world.

Recent studies on the baby-boomer generation reveal that many people choose to continue working rather than retire. There are several reasons for this, such as improved health or enjoyment of what they are doing. But one of the main reasons is financial need. David Callahan, author of *The American Prospect*, said, "Some 3.3 million seniors still live below the poverty line. Several million more scrape by just above the poverty line. For many of these people, poverty is the reward for adult lives spent continuously in the workforce or raising children and managing a family."

So make sure that you plan your future with your eyes wide open. The time to create a financial blueprint for your family, and to start building long-term wealth, is now. Ideally, you want your personal assets to continuously work on your behalf so that your income stream isn't dependent on putting in a certain number of hours each workday. What you choose to do with your time is something you can control. That is true financial and physical freedom.

**Creating a Wealthy Mindset**

We have all grown up with certain biases toward wealth and money, and they subconsciously affect our ability to attract and maintain wealth. The sad thing is that many of us have a negative bias and don't realize it. There is an abundance of opportunities in the world for creating wealth, and they are accessible to everyone. But they might as well be located in outer space for people living with a scarcity mentality.

It is the opposite of a wealthy mindset: a person living with a subconscious belief in scarcity won't bother looking for an opportunity to increase their circumstances. They will believe that everything has already been picked over, like the last fruit on a grocer's stand. This type of negative bias will actually push people farther away from financial freedom. They'll make excuses and explain that being wealthy is a bad thing; the status quo will be justified.

Wealth and success go hand in hand, involving very similar attitudes. Most people don't like reaching past their comfort zone and taking the risks required to achieve great success. So they create excuses based on circular logic to explain why they are still in their current situation. In contrast, wealthy individuals are always moving forward, taking action and risks that bring them closer to succeeding in their personal or professional goals.

Popular fiction often portrays wealthy, successful people as selfish, stingy hoarders, but quite the opposite is true. Wealthy people not only amass great wealth for themselves and their family but are often very generous to others, especially those who are less fortunate. Because of their financial resources, they are able to make a real difference in the world. Newspapers and magazines devoted to philanthropy are filled with the names and activities of affluent individuals and families who are busy making a difference in causes that are important to them.

You often hear people say that money isn't everything and they don't need it to be happy. In reality, nobody can live without it. Money is essential to survival in today's world. Even if your goals aren't defined by dollar amounts, you need a certain amount of money to live a comfortable lifestyle and achieve your dreams.

Rather than viewing money as good or bad, think of it as a vehicle that can be exchanged for your goals. For example, creating multiple streams of passive income can make it possible for you to spend more quality time with your family. In this case, it isn't the money that makes you happy but how it creates freedom to control your day.

### Leslie's Wealth-Creation Strategy

I have a large extended family and we are all in different phases of our lives. The one creative thing that my family does is hold monthly "wealth creation meetings." Regardless of where we are in our personal lives, we find these meetings beneficial because it gives us a chance to learn and grow together. After all, it can get quite lonely climbing the ladder of success without your loved ones. During these meetings, we discuss topics such as financial literacy, goal setting, problem solving, and even share specific opportunities.

These meetings are a reflection of my passion for life-long learning, which is another component of the mindset that you need to develop to become a successful real estate investor. There are many books and courses that will help you develop your financial literacy and wealth mindset.

I would like to note one resource in particular. In Chapter One, I described reading the book *Rich Dad Poor Dad* by Robert Kiyosaki and Sharon Lechter. This book describes how investing in real estate and owning your own business can help you to create wealth. There is a Rich Dad Education series based on the book that includes the Learn to Be Rich and Launch Your Business courses. Free information seminars are held in many communities, providing an overview of a course's contents. Visit www.richdadeducation.com for more information.

Another source for developing your financial literacy is an organization aimed at real estate investors. As Canadian-based investors, we have found that the Real Estate Investment Network (REIN) is one of the best organizations. However, in the same way that our successful, proprietary strategy is an international process that gets results, you can search out similar networks in other countries—or become a founder of one if it doesn't exist.

Not only do I amass valuable knowledge and updates from REIN, but I have also had the pleasure of meeting hundreds of other like-minded investors who share a common passion. (See Chapter Seven for more information on networking with other investors.)

**Capitalize on a Slow-Moving Market**

The real estate market moves slowly in comparison to other types of investments, offering you a lot of time to understand and respond to its fluctuations. Unlike the stock market, which can have major fluctuations on a daily basis, the real estate market will often show signs of change long before the impact

is felt. Astute investors know this and look for factors affecting the real estate market in the areas where they are investing.

For example, the recent sub-prime crisis in the United States should not have come as a great surprise to a sophisticated investor. There were indications of the upcoming collapse of the housing market long before the impact was actually felt. A financially shrewd investor with a long-term plan would have anticipated it, and would have been prepared to weather the storm.

These are turbulent times and there has been a lot of fear among the general public as a reaction to issues such as the sub-prime meltdown and the general state of the economy. But Avner Mandelman, in an excellent article at Globeadvisor.com, states, "When risks are most visible, not only are they on the way to being addressed, but the panic they generate often causes otherwise sane people to dump perfectly good stocks for next to nothing. Therefore, the scarier the headlines and the riskier the world seems, the more likely it is that problems are in the process of being solved."

Getting past the fear and continuing to take action is important to your mindset as a successful investor. Even with the expected, cyclical nature of the real estate market, a well-managed portfolio can weather the storm. This includes well-researched investments with built-in, adequate reserves, located in areas with strong economic fundamentals. Keeping your properties well managed also includes ensuring that they are fully rented out. In this way, even in a slow or declining market, your properties are still bringing in cash flow, month after month.

We should be aware that times like this offer many good real estate opportunities. Even though most people understand the theory of buy-low-sell-high, they often do not follow this logic. In a panic, they often dump properties in an attempt to minimize their losses. Being able to hold on through tough markets, and not panic with the masses, permits you to take advantage of the many deals that arise due to inexperienced investors dumping their properties at an inopportune time.

## About Investment Diversification

Adding real estate to an existing financial portfolio helps to build long-term wealth by offering greater diversity to your nest egg. Since all investment vehicles are cyclical, choosing different types of investments can help you capitalize on this fact. While one area of your portfolio might be hitting a low, another investment may be in a growth period at the same time and will be able to offset any losses. In contrast, putting all your eggs into one basket can put you at risk of losing everything if the market for your sole investment falls.

You can diversify further by holding different types of properties in different geographical areas (see Chapter Five for more information). You may initially feel most comfortable investing in your own backyard. As your confidence grows, you can expand into other parts of the country, and then into many promising international regions. Chapter Nine offers more tips on creating wealth by growing your real estate investment portfolio.

Eventually, you can use our successful, proprietary strategy to evaluate any property anywhere in the world. This book offers Canadian examples of an international process that gets results. Just be sure to follow our steps to properly analyze and identify potential investments with strong economic fundamentals.

## The Basics of Financial Statements

Successful investors have a clear picture of their financial situation and monitor how they are doing, year after year. Without knowing where you stand financially, it is difficult to measure your success over time.

Financial statements provide an important baseline by which you can measure and compare all future actions to your bottom line. By understanding your starting point, you will be able to tie it to your long-term goals and set specific milestones that make sense rather than picking random numbers out of the air.

In addition, as an investor you will likely be looking for mortgages for acquiring your properties. Understanding and presenting your financial statements to potential lenders will be a vital key to securing the loans you need. They are a necessary starting point in understanding where you stand in the eyes of a potential lender and will form the basis of clear communication with your support network.

The balance sheet provides a snapshot of a company's financial position. Its assets appear on the left; its liabilities and owners' equity are on the right. This reflects a fundamental accounting equation where Owners' Equity (or Net Worth) = Assets – Liabilities (or Net Assets). The assets are listed in the order in which they can be converted into cash. Liabilities appear in the order they can be liquidated. This ranking shows whether a company is positioned to effectively meet its short-term obligations. The balance sheet also shows a company's leverage: the ratio between capital lent by creditors and the capital supplied by its owners.

Here's a simple example of how this data is used. An investor may state the financial goal of having $1 million. On the surface, that may seem impressive. However, it is important to clarify what is meant by that statement. For example, does the person want to have $1 million in assets, a net worth of $1 million, or annual revenue of $1 million? All three goals revolve around having $1 million but the meanings are very different. Having a net worth of $1 million is much more impressive than having $1 million in assets if your balance sheet is heavy on the liabilities side.

A company's profit-and-loss statement, also known as an income statement, is another key financial statement. It is like a report card on the company's activities, presenting its net income or net loss relative to retained earnings over a set fiscal period. It includes intermediary calculations of income, including gross income, operating income, and pre-tax income, which are crucial to the task of analyzing a company's operations.

## Sample Balance Sheet/Net Worth Statement
(as at December 31, 2008)

| ASSETS | | LIABILITIES | |
|---|---|---|---|
| **Bank Accounts** | | **Mortgages** | |
| Checking Accounts | 1,000 | Principal Residence | 300,000 |
| Savings Account | 5,000 | Rental Portfolio | 1,500,000 |
| Other Savings Accounts | 3,000 | | |
| Canada Savings Bond | 1,000 | TOTAL Mortgages | $1,800,000 |
| | | | |
| TOTAL Deposit Accounts | $10,000 | **Loans** | |
| | | Loan 1 | 20,000 |
| **Investments** (Registered & Unregistered Funds) | | | |
| Group RRSP Partner 1 | 50,000 | TOTAL Loans | $20,000 |
| ABC Mutual Funds | 3,000 | | |
| XYZ Mutual Funds | 10,000 | **Accounts Payable** | |
| Group RRSP Partner 2 | 80,000 | Visa | 3,000 |
| Other RRSP Partner 2 | 10,000 | MasterCard | 1,200 |
| Canadian Scholarship Trust | 3,000 | American Express | 800 |
| | | | |
| TOTAL Investments | $156,000 | TOTAL Accounts Payable | $5,000 |
| | | | |
| Real Estate Portfolio | | | |
| Rental Property Portfolio (see appendix) | 2,000,000 | | |
| Principal Residence | 500,000 | | |
| | | | |
| TOTAL Real Estate Portfolio | $2,500,000 | | |
| | | | |
| **Goods and Chattels** | | | |
| Vehicle 1 | 10,000 | | |
| Vehicle 2 | 5,000 | | |
| Personal Property | 10,000 | | |
| Equipment | 7,500 | | |
| | | | |
| TOTAL Goods and Chattels | $32,500 | | |
| | | | |
| **TOTAL ASSETS** | **$2,698,500** | **TOTAL LIABILITIES** | **$1,825,000** |

**Net Worth = $ 873,500**

## Sample Income Statement
### (for the month ended December 31, 2008)

### INCOME

| Income | Monthly | Totals |
|---|---|---|
| Revenue property rental income  (See Appendix) | 12,000 | |
| Employment income – partner 1 | 8,000 | |
| Employment income – partner 2 | 14,000 | |
| **Total Income Per Month** | | **$34,000** |

### EXPENSES

| Regular Monthly Expenses | Monthly | Totals |
|---|---|---|
| Revenue property debt servicing | 10,153 | |
| Revenue property operating expenses | 7,200 | |
| Principal residence mortgage | 1,693 | |
| Utilities: heat, light, basic telephone rental, cable television | 500 | |
| Automobile transportation: gasoline, maintenance, parking | 400 | |
| Groceries and other household supplies | 500 | |
| Clothing: including work clothes, sportswear, repairs, accessories | 250 | |
| Medical & dental care:<br>    including prescription drugs and deductible expenses | 100 | |
| Consumer credit payments:<br>    credit cards and secured lines of credit | 300 | |
| Other personal spending:<br>    grooming aids, haircuts, dry cleaning, etc. | 100 | **$21,196** |

| Discretionary Spending | Monthly | Totals |
|---|---|---|
| Educational expenses: daycare & tuition | 1,000 | |
| Entertainment:<br>    dining, theater tickets, printed materials, etc. | 200 | |
| Gifts:<br>    special occasions, charitable donations, etc. | 35 | |
| Miscellaneous:<br>    long distance phone/fax calls, lunches & snacks, indulgences | 100 | **$ 1,335** |

| Occasional Expenses (including regular non-monthly payments) | Monthly | Totals |
|---|---|---|
| Home/apartment insurance: paid annually | 50 | |
| Auto insurance & life insurance: paid monthly | 425 | |
| Recreational and/or club memberships: paid monthly | 32 | **$507** |

| | | |
|---|---|---|
| **Total Expenses Per Month** | | **$23,038** |

| | | |
|---|---|---|
| **MONTHLY RESIDUAL INCOME (Before Taxes):** | | **$10,962** |

# Chapter Five

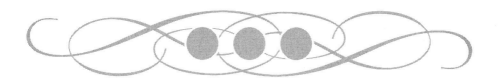

## *Location, Location:*

### WHERE TO BUILD YOUR WEALTH

The next five chapters of *R3: Real People with Real Strategies for Real Estate Investing* will outline our successful process for planning, selecting, and acquiring investment properties. You will discover how to complete the essential research, or due diligence, before initiating a purchase; how to arrange the most optimal financing; how to direct to your advantage the steps involved in closing a deal; how to work with your network of contacts to support your success; and how to strategically manage your portfolio of investments to increase your wealth.

Although the goals for acquiring real estate can vary, we find that careful planning always produces the most success for investors. This planning begins with detailed area research to verify that we will be investing in a region that is economically strong and poised for future growth. It is only after making this determination that we begin the process of selecting and analyzing specific properties (this will be discussed in Chapter Six).

**Leslie Illustrates the Importance of Area Research**

Based on my experience, gathering information about an area from multiple sources has proven to be very important. After acquiring my first two local properties, I began investing in property outside of the province I reside in. I visited the area and found one that was priced well, showed good numbers, and had positive cash flow. It already had tenants in place and, although it appeared messy during our visits, was structurally in good condition.

As we drove around, the neighborhood seemed fairly quiet; the homes were well kept; and according to some of our team members, it was a decent area. Based on the feedback we received and the basic homework we had done, it appeared to be a good opportunity. As a result, we proceeded to purchase this property.

However, not long after the purchase, things began to go wrong. We had trouble finding and keeping quality tenants, our property was vandalized, and several nagging issues kept arising. After talking to more investors and new team members, we realized that, although the neighborhood was in transition, it may have been one of the worst neighborhoods we could have invested in.

There are two lessons to be learned here. The first is to be more thorough than I was. Had we taken the time to get those second opinions before purchasing the property, we could have saved ourselves a lot of grief. They might have conflicted with the first opinions we received, but this is valuable in itself. Although there is never a perfect answer or ideal time or place

to invest, you can limit your risk by taking the time to verify and understand why different sources have conflicting opinions.

The second is to listen carefully and take the time to understand conflicting sources. You may often get several viewpoints, depending on who you talk to. With this in mind, make sure to absorb all feedback and then verify the information by doing your own research. Once you have all the information, it becomes your responsibility to decide on whether it is a good investment.

## Economic Fundamentals

Understanding economic fundamentals is an important part of becoming a successful real estate investor. You should have a solid grasp of what is happening in an area where you are planning to invest. Don't get caught up in only looking at past performance. You need to be concerned about what the future holds for that area. Specifically, look for cities or towns that are poised for future growth, with economic development offices actively involved in attracting business into the region.

The amount of information you will have access to may seem overwhelming. However, once you develop a system of information gathering, and begin to understand the factors that will impact your investment, you will be able to identify statistics and figures that are useful for determining whether or not to begin investing in a region. Our philosophy has always been to keep it simple. We usually begin with basic information gathering by doing the following:

- read the local papers to get a feel for the community;

- visit or call the local economic development office and ask how they plan to attract business and people to their city/town;

- visit the local planning department to find out what infrastructure improvements are currently taking place or are planned for the future;

- do research online. For example, to get a feel for the local housing market on Canadian cities, visit www.cmhc.ca or visit www.statisticscanada.com for information on demographics. To get information on American cities, visit www.hud.gov regarding the housing market or www.census.gov for information on demographics;

- join a local investment club or business club to make potentially useful connections;

- talk to other investors who already invest in that area.

Certain key factors will help you to gather the right information and correctly interpret the results of your research. These include: the basic economics of supply and demand; area demographics and understanding forecasts and trends; determining the cycles of the local real estate market; recognizing an area's political climate and how it will impact your investment; evaluating the infrastructure, both existing and planned; and identifying a desirable location.

### The Law of Supply and Demand

Economics, as defined by Princeton University's WordNet Web site (wordnet.princeton.edu), is "the branch of social science that deals with the production and distribution and consumption of goods and services and their management." As with any other type of goods, real estate is impacted by the laws of supply and demand. A basic understanding of economics will assist you in making informed decisions when analyzing a particular area or opportunity.

This can offer valuable perspectives about the type of investment strategy you choose. Recognizing how these laws work and how they affect the real estate market will help you in timing your purchases and sales. In addition, understanding the underlying mechanisms that drive the real estate market will allow you to read between the lines and come to your own conclusions about what is really happening.

It is easy to be swayed by what is portrayed in the media. Being able to separate facts from headlines will allow you to make more informed decisions. Rather than focusing on the negative gloom and doom, focus on the trends that are being depicted and the opportunities that present themselves during these periods.

As with any investment, real estate goes through cycles that are a result of changes in consumer opinion. As an investor, you need to be aware of how this affects the housing market in the areas you invest in. We are not suggesting that you become an economist. Rather, we encourage you to understand the basic laws of supply and demand. This way, when you read or listen to economic forecasts and updates, you will have a better understanding of the mechanisms behind the changes that are occurring or are being predicted.

Here is a very brief summary of these two principles. The law of demand states that there is an inverse relationship between the price of a good and the amount of the good that buyers will purchase. For example, as prices start rising, other things being constant, consumer demand starts declining.

The law of supply states that there is a direct relationship between the price of a good and the amount of the good offered for sale. Therefore, as the price of a product increases, other things being constant, suppliers will attempt to maximize profits by increasing the quantity of the product sold.

The following positive depiction, from American billionaire and real estate tycoon Sam Zell, shows how economic trends and real estate are tightly linked. "Interest rates are going to go up because employment is going to go up. If employment goes up, then our apartments get filled. And if employment goes up, our office buildings get filled. The reality is that increased economic activity combined with increased interest rates is basically bullish for real estate."

## Demographics

Demographics are the characteristics of a particular population, such as age, race, gender, income, and education. It is important to know the population characteristics within the area you plan to invest in because the types of properties that are in demand and the strategies you employ depend on a population's wants and needs. Groups that share common characteristics, such as baby boomers, tend to make similar consumer choices.

A city or town with a mature population will have very different housing needs than one with a younger population because these groups are at different stages in their lives. Within a mature population, you may find that there is a trend toward downsizing and a demand for smaller bungalows that are easy to maintain or condos that cater to an aging population. Their children have most likely left the family home to create families of their own, and retirees may want to spend more time travelling or enjoying hobbies that they didn't have time for while working and raising families. In this case, finding a property that requires little maintenance may be of utmost importance.

On the flip side, a younger population can drive growth in single-family homes or be receptive to lease-to-own opportunities in their community. Young couples or families are at a phase in their lives where they are looking to purchase their first homes. They may be having children and expanding their families so they may desire to expand into larger homes.

Those are just some examples of the ways you can interpret the changing demographics in a region. Once you take the time to identify and understand the groups within the area you are investing in, you can come to your own conclusions.

The Canadian Mortgage and Housing Corporation hosts seminars that provide useful information and forecasts for a region; similar organizations in other countries might do the same. If you are actively investing in a region, we highly recommend that you attend such events on a regular basis or subscribe to newsletters that can help you to stay on top of upcoming trends.

### Local Real Estate Market

Although you may have a good grasp of what is happening on a national level, you need to focus on the local real estate market where you plan to invest. This is especially true when investing in an area outside of where you currently live. As British property developer Sarah Beeny says, "Before you start trying to work out which direction the property market is headed, you should be aware that there are markets within markets."

What is happening within a specific region can be very different from what is happening on a national level. Often, when you watch the news or read national newspapers, you are getting input on the average of what is happening across the country. However, the situation can be very different from one town to another. Make sure to get specific facts on the area you are targeting.

You can get this information by reading local newspapers and talking to local realtors and other investors. You can also join a local real estate investment club or organization that specializes in the type of property you plan to purchase.

### Political Climate

Be active in understanding the local political climate. Are the community leaders friendly to investors and business owners? If not, speak up and participate in encouraging local politicians to promote investor-friendly initiatives.

### Infrastructure

It is not enough for a city or town to actively promote growth and try to attract investment and new business. It must also prepare for that growth. We have visited small towns with outstanding growth projections that have no plans to accommodate the increased population. Down the road, this can result in a frustrating environment for residents and a decline in the area's desirability.

Infrastructure changes, such as new roads, bridges, airports, and sewers, are signs of well-planned growth. Such improvements can have a positive impact on the surrounding areas. The enhanced accessibility, shortened travel times, reduced traffic congestion, and many other benefits reflect a greater ability to accommodate a growing population. This can have a positive impact on the real estate market. By knowing what is happening today, and what is planned over the next few years, you can forecast the impact on your investments.

### Location

Using our step-by-step process, you can successfully evaluate any property in any location in the world. This will allow you to diversify your portfolio by holding investments in different geographical areas that appeal to you. Start by doing the due diligence that identifies a city or town with the solid economic fundamentals that make you want to invest there. Next, consider what neighborhoods indicate the best prospects for investing.

The quality of your property and the tenants you are able to attract will largely depend on where your investment is located in the community. For example, if you select a property in a transitional area, it may be priced very well. However, it may not be as easy to attract the type of quality tenants you would like to have, and you must ensure that this area is positioned to transition profitably.

You can often tell a lot about a neighborhood by driving around and looking at how the properties are maintained. If you aren't familiar with an area, find an investor who is. Ask him or her to tell you about the different parts of the city before you make your decision. A good realtor will be able to provide you with an abundance of information and tips on pockets within the city.

## A Template for Creating Your Own Area Study

With the above factors in mind, summarizing and understanding the information you collect will be central to your success. The conclusions you draw from actively interpreting what you learn will assist you in making educated investment decisions. Asking good questions will help you to develop this ability.

An area study should be as detailed as possible. Don't hesitate to contact newspaper sources, municipal officials, politicians, and local real estate professionals to find out what they know. People are often very happy to display their knowledge and this can work to your advantage. Keep careful notes from your conversations with these professionals. As well, your area study should include any reports or forecasts you can gather from local economic development offices.

Here are some things to look for during your investigation, and the types of information to gather:

- a diverse economy, not dependent on any one major employer

- demonstrated economic growth over the last few years

- active and business-friendly economic development office

- strong and specific growth plan in place to attract businesses to the region and accommodate future expansion

- demographics reflecting a young population; population growth that is surpassing the national average; high rate of immigration

- a region where the median income is higher than the national average

- low unemployment rate

- forecasts of what will be in demand over the next few years in that area based on demographics, sales trends, etc.

- historical housing prices and past cycles, vacancy rates, and the percentage of housing that is owner-occupied vs. rental dwelling

- political climate: if there is an investor- and landlord-friendly local government

- what kind of restrictions are in place for the types of investments you are looking into (for example, many areas have restrictions or limitations with regard to student rentals)

- plans for major transportation improvements and infrastructure such as new roads and bridges that will allow easier access into and within the area; look at projected infrastructure change as well as what is currently happening

- the community's proximity to airports, train stations, and other transportation

- existence of adequate schools and future plans for schools to accommodate growth plans

- the amenities currently in place and in the planning stage

- available health care facilities

74

After doing your initial research, keep in mind that things are always changing so it is important to stay up-to-date with what is happening in the areas you are investing in. As we have stated before, knowledge is power. The more informed you are, the better poised you will be to make profitable and timely investment decisions that take full advantage of opportunities when they arise.

Once your due diligence has identified an area or community with solid economic fundamentals, you will be ready to evaluate specific properties. Chapter Six will discuss the steps involved in acquiring the kind of real estate that promises a profitable return on your investment.

WWW.R3BOOK.COM

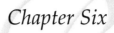

*Chapter Six*

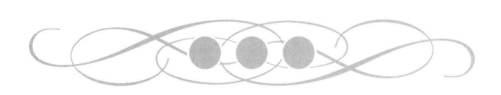

*The Appreciation Potential:*

EVALUATING PROPERTY

*"I always liked the idea that a group of people would pool their money together to pay off the mortgage on my building…that they would give me extra money at the end of the month that I could use to reinvest, put into a savings account, or just have some fun with."*
— Harry Helmsley

The next steps in your careful planning will concern the type of investment property you will acquire. However, before looking into specific properties, you must begin by defining the strategy you will employ as an investor. The approach you take will depend on what you are trying to accomplish.

Are you looking for a steady stream of passive income? Or are you looking for a short-term, highly profitable venture where you will pull out all your capital and profits within a year? It is important to establish such specific investment criteria. This includes taking into account your planned exit strategy.

Generally speaking, the higher a project's forecasted rate of return, the more desirable it is to undertake the project. But this is usually associated with a higher risk level. So consider your level of risk tolerance and the type of return you expect to see.

You may initially feel most comfortable acquiring property in your own backyard. But you can also apply the solid investment principles in our proprietary strategy to other regions throughout the world. Simply ensure that your target area is showing the strong economic fundamentals we discussed in Chapter Five.

Your starting point as an investor will also be dictated by how much capital you have available to use as a down payment. However, you can make your finances go a lot farther by using leverage. As we discussed in Chapter Four, real estate's value as a tangible asset means that leverage is more available than with other investments. Remember that you must carry the higher payments resulting from this larger debt load if your property goes vacant during the real estate cycle. Planning for such expenses is part of our analysis process for evaluating different types of investment properties. In this chapter, we include sample calculations to assist you with projecting your costs and cash flow.

By clearly defining your criteria for selecting investment property, you can sift through the opportunities and concentrate on those that correspond to your goal. Remaining focused on the objectives you set for yourself is part of developing your mindset of success as an investor.

Your specifics will also help in communicating with your network—the people who will be assisting you along the way (see Chapter Eight for more information). For example, we typically provide a one-page summary to our realtor contacts to help them understand exactly what opportunities we want to look at. With this information, they will be better able to select appropriate listings to send our way.

Below is the criteria list we put together for a recent commercial property search in southern Ontario. It outlines the key features we are looking for, such as price point, location, and building specifications. It is essentially a wish list for our next acquisition. Don't hesitate to create a similar list to outline your ideal investment opportunity. This kind of clear communication is far more likely to produce results than providing an open-ended or vague description.

# Commercial Property Search Criteria

Meridian Commercial Investments Inc. is looking to acquire two to three commercial properties over the next 12 to 18 months.

## General Investment Criteria

Purpose: To acquire commercial real estate that will provide steady income for our investors (to be distributed as annual dividends) and long-term capital growth (initial capital is to be recovered via refinancing, once building value is increased, and/or from the sale of the property)

Building Quality: Quality product of Class A to B

Purchase Price: Under $2.5 million

Financing: Prefer some seller financing if possible

Size: Up to 30,000 square feet

Location: Hamilton, Brantford, Burlington, or surrounding areas

Vacancy: 10% vacant or less

Desired Cap Rate: 10% or better, or reasonable cash-on-cash return, based upon existing revenue, with upside potential through vacancy factors and lease rollovers.

Other: Good parking ratios, traffic counts, and access. Close to major roadways/highways and public transit lines.

## Additional Criteria by Property Type

Multi-unit industrial:
- preferably already divided with multiple tenants
- truck-level or grade-level shipping/loading docks
- adequate parking for all tenants and a lot large enough to accommodate incoming shipping trucks, etc.

## Office building:
- preferably professional/medical buildings
- demographics indicating a middle-class population of at least 100,000 within a 15-minute drive to the building
- adequate parking for tenants and their clients

## Retail plaza:
- strong anchor and/or national tenants
- demographics indicating a middle-class population of at least 100,000 within a 15-minute drive to the plaza
- excellent visibility, with access to the plaza from a main roadway
- adequate parking for tenants and customers

## Multi-family townhome complex or higher-end condo/apartment style building with potential for condo conversion:
- demographics indicating middle-income neighborhood
- located near all amenities: schools, transit, shopping, etc.
- good unit mix (prefer a combination of 2- to 3-bedroom units)
- adequate parking for all tenants and visitors

**Buying Pre-Construction**

If you drive through the outlying regions of most urban areas, you will see signs promoting a new subdivision development, but they will be sitting at the edge of an undeveloped tract of land. Other than that colorful sign and a parking lot with a sales center, there will be no other indication that construction is underway. However, a marketing program will likely be in progress to lure buyers to the barren site, usually with attractive early-bird incentive pricing.

Pre-selling homes in new developments is a standard practice that allows developers to secure purchaser commitments before the construction phase begins. You can often buy a pre-construction home at a lower price than it will be worth by the time you take possession many months later.

There are two reasons for this. First, the developer needs to pre-sell a percentage of the homes to borrow the money to start construction. So you can get a lower price if you commit to buying in the pre-construction phase. Second, in an upward-moving market, you can benefit from the appreciation in value even before the home's closing date arrives.

Pre-construction homes can be a great investment if purchased in the right area and at the right price. The home's value will usually increase once it is completed, which allows you to either sell it at a profit or retain it as an investment by lining up potential tenants or lease-to-own candidates.

The process of making this purchase is simple, but very critical. You begin by meeting with the developer (or a sales agent) to discuss the price and review the contract legalities. Make sure that you are fully aware of all that is expected, both from you and from the developer, in the construction of your home. It is a good idea to have your real estate lawyer review the contract and provide you with advice.

As an investor, it is also important to research the developer as much as possible. Your network of contacts can help you with this. Ensure that the developer is reputable, with many years of experience in new home construction. You can avoid construction nightmares down the road by buying from a developer with a well-established reputation for quality and reliability.

We have seen newer, smaller builders try to enter an active market where buyer demand is much greater than the planned supply of homes can satisfy. In an effort to profit from the market upswing, they try to capitalize on their construction skills by assuming the role of a developer. However, due to lack of experience or improper management, many of these small builders go out of business, leaving the purchaser hanging.

Although pre-construction opportunities can be seen as speculative, they can also be very profitable. By locking in the price in an upward-moving market, you are able to watch your future investment property grow in value even before you close the deal.

## Fixer-Uppers

You can often find properties for sale, well below market value, because they need repair work. Sellers who desire a quick sale will often reduce the price and offer a property "as is" to get rid of it in a timely manner. People shopping for their own home may have difficulty seeing past the appearance to what it could be, or they want to buy a home that is fully ready for them to move in.

As an investor, the uglier a home appears, the better it can be for you. These types of properties can become profitable if you can acquire them at a good discount and stay within your renovation budget. (Doing a repair-cost plan, which is absolutely essential, is discussed in detail later in this chapter.)

Keep in mind that you will be paying taxes on any profits from the sale of this investment property. Proper tax planning with

a qualified accountant is essential to ensuring that the project will be worthwhile. The proceeds will either be taxed as capital gains or business income depending on your personal situation and how the transaction is assessed.

### Foreclosures and Tax Sales

A foreclosure property is a property that becomes available after a person defaults on their mortgage contract. When they cannot afford to pay back the mortgage, the lender has the right to sell the property and recover what is owed on it. Many investors like to buy foreclosed homes because they are usually sold at a discounted price. The hardest part about investing in foreclosure properties is finding them. A good strategy involves getting to know real estate agents in your target vicinity.

A tax-sale property is a property that has been taken over by the city or town it is located in because its owner did not pay the property taxes. Depending on the city or town, these homes are often auctioned off. The tax-sale procedure varies with each municipality so get in touch with the local government to get the required information before proceeding.

### Multi-Family Building/Apartment Complex

This is the advanced category in residential investment property because of its magnitude compared to a single dwelling. The opportunities that come with it are on a similar scale. The only real difference between these two investments is the level of profit, or return on investment (ROI), that can be expected, and the degree of risk. With a multi-family complex, the investor is able to buy in volume. It can be compared to buying something wholesale versus retail.

When carefully planned, a multi-unit apartment complex offers considerable ROI potential in return for the risk involved. During times of low interest rates, demand for apartment rentals tends to be low but it will increase as interest rates rise. In addition, apartments can be offered for sale instead of for rent, or converted into condominiums. Timing is also important with regard to this kind of purchase. You could receive one or two months' rent upon closing, as well as any security deposits held by the previous landlord, but you may not have to make your first loan payment for several weeks.

Apartment complexes should have a good history of rental income and vacancy rates for you to review. If possible, obtain copies of maintenance records as well. Larger complexes may be managed by a property management company.

### Commercial Property

Commercial property includes office buildings, retail space (including strip malls), industrial space, medical centers, and hotels. When investigating a property, be sure to consider its highest and best use; for example, it is possible to rezone a residential dwelling, which is located on a busy street, into a more valuable commercial property.

There are several key differences between this type of investment and a residential property. The value of a residential property is based on the sale of comparable buildings. Whatever a tenant pays you in rent won't affect its value. But a commercial property's worth is directly based on net income. You can boost the value of this real estate by bringing in a tenant who pays higher rent.

Therefore, the higher the rent—and the higher the quality of the tenant—the more your building is worth. Alternatively, you can increase your net income by keeping control over and/or reducing your expenses. For example, you can renegotiate property management or service contract fees.

Commercial property owners welcome much longer leases because they can enhance the property's value. A government office or large corporate tenant is considered a "blue chip" tenant. They are likely to rent the property for much longer periods of up to 20 years, and are unlikely to default on the rent.

On the downside, in return for having the tenant sign a long-term commercial lease, you may be locked into smaller annual rental increases. The specified contractual increase may be less than what the market could bear if you were to lease the unit to a new tenant.

Because the look and condition of the property is important to their business and staff, commercial tenants tend to spend more on maintaining the property. However, costs such as elevator and air conditioning maintenance, roof repairs, and operating expenses will be a lot higher than in a residential investment.

**Land**

Land can be a solid investment as long as you do your homework. A major factor that determines its value is the location. Twenty acres of land in the middle of nowhere might only cost $20,000, while that same lot near a big city like New York or Los Angeles could be worth millions. The same can be said for land near rivers, lakes, or oceans. People like to live close to the water and are willing to pay more for that luxury.

As an investment, land gives you plenty of options for its use. You can build a residential development or turn it into a commercial complex. Some investors simply buy land and hold it. They rent it to local farmers to cover the monthly carrying costs, and sell it many years later at a higher price.

Do your research to avoid buying land that is contaminated from an oil leakage or other prior use. The cost of doing an environmental cleanup can far outweigh its value. Be sure to

check with the local environmental protection office and the board of health regarding any suspected contamination. If necessary, have the land surveyed for possible contamination before entering into an agreement to purchase.

### Leslie's Tax-Sale Caution

When I first started purchasing residential investment property, I tried to keep emotion out of it and focused strictly on the research: the economic fundamentals of an area and a property's potential income and profitability. I spent a lot of time determining where I wanted to invest and the type of properties I wanted to acquire only to discover that, no matter how much I tried to keep emotion out of real estate investing, it finds a way to creep back in.

You will sometimes find emotion in the form of a gut feeling that effectively guides your choices. However, in many cases, emotion becomes a factor because there are other people involved. Your relationship with sellers, joint-venture partners, and team members will always bring the emotional and human side of investing to the forefront.

When I was looking for creative ways to find motivated sellers, I began by investigating tax sales. This situation, where an owner hasn't made property tax payments over a certain period of time, seemed like a profitable opportunity. But I was only looking at the numbers. I hadn't realized the amount of pain the seller could be in, or how much this could affect me.

Buying tax-sale properties is a strategy that some investors use to acquire property that is usually well below market value. Many investors then flip the property for a quick profit. The way in which tax sales are run varies from town to town, but in essence the municipality takes over the property and sells it at auction.

After taking a course on tax sales, I figured that the best way to go about it was offering help to a homeowner before the

actual tax sale took place. Depending on their situation, I thought that it would be easy enough to work out a fair transaction that was beneficial to both of us.

So I went through the list of tax-sale properties in an area that I was planning to invest in. Then I drove past the ones that were of interest to me to get a feel for the neighborhood and the condition of the property. After narrowing my list down to two properties, I went to the land registry office and pulled title on them to get the owners' names. I could only find contact information for one of the owners in the local phonebook. Armed with a point-form list of the benefits that I could offer, I picked up the phone to make my first call.

I was admittedly a little nervous about talking with a complete stranger to discuss a very sensitive topic: coming close to losing one's home. I wondered what the reaction would be to my stepping in at this point. Would he or she realize that I truly wanted to create a win-win situation, or would I be seen as a vulture trying to take advantage?

An elderly woman, whose quiet voice quavered as she spoke, answered the phone. I introduced myself and my company, then gently mentioned the impending tax sale of her home. It became very quiet on the other end. I heard her crying; and I felt awful about being so in-her-face during such a personal time.

I slowly tried to explain how I could help her out. She just kept repeating that she didn't understand what was happening and didn't want to lose the home she'd lived in for so many years. I asked if she had family that could help her and offered to contact them to explain what I was suggesting, if that would be easier for her. She said her husband had passed away a few years before and had always handled their finances; she had no family that would be willing or able to help her.

By this point I was nearly in tears myself. It took everything I had to keep on telling her that, by doing nothing, she could lose her home within the week.

In business, all that I do comes from a sense of integrity and a sincere desire to help others. I'm not in the game to hustle or take advantage of people, but to creatively make the most of profitable situations. So I wasn't trying to push her; I just wanted to ensure that she understood the severity of the situation. Her position was desperate and I feared that someone else might contact her and ruthlessly exploit her situation. I wanted to be fair in dealing with her, and it was making me feel just awful.

Finally, she was too upset and politely told me that she had to go and didn't need my help. I thanked her for taking the time to listen to me and gave my name and phone number in case she changed her mind. I never heard back from her; when I tried to follow up a few days later, no one answered the phone. On the day of the tax sale, I submitted my sealed bid but didn't secure the property. It went to the highest bidder and I don't know what happened to her.

This experience made me realize that real estate investing is not just a series of steps or transactions. To acquire properties creatively, you have to think outside the box and stand out from the crowd, but there is far more to it than the numbers and the process. From the unfortunate lady in the tax-sale situation to problem tenants to building rapport with your team members, the ability to work with people and nurture these relationships is an important part of the equation.

This business is about working with people, which is why I offer my investors or clients the best value and service I can. It's about listening to others while communicating well enough for people to hear what I have to say. Investing in real estate is about people and the bonds you build with them.

**Property Analysis**

We have come to the point where you have identified an area that has the solid economic fundamentals we discussed in

Chapter Five, and found some promising cities or towns that are poised for future growth. You have determined what type of property you would like to invest in. Now it's time to start looking at specific properties.

Before making a purchase, doing a thorough property analysis helps to determine that your potential investment can support all future expenses including the debt service. This is absolutely critical in running a profitable portfolio. We cannot emphasize strongly enough that, in this (and almost any other) business, *cash flow is king!*

Before getting started, you must collect some essential information, which may come from the seller, your realtor, or your own research.

- *Begin with a verification of income or potential income.* If the property is currently a rental property, you can request a copy of all rental agreements to see what income it generates. If it is not currently tenanted, ask your realtor to give you comparables on rental units in the area. You can also go through local real estate or online classifieds to determine rental rates in the area. Keep in mind that a vacancy is likely to occur at some point; try to determine the local vacancy rate to factor into your calculation.

- *You must also do a verification of expenses.* The seller can give you a summary of the historical property expenses. You will need to know the costs for insurance (but also get a current quote from your insurance agent), property taxes, advertising, property management, repairs and maintenance, and so forth. Be conservative in your estimates; you will want to anticipate future increases in your expenses.

Use this data to build a solid reserve into your calculations, based on your estimate of what it will cost to cover repairs, maintenance, and possible vacancies. It will alleviate any financial strain because these expenses are already planned for. As well, discuss your plans with your lender and determine the debt-service payments; make sure that the monthly rental income can also cover this.

Below are examples of two investment properties that I currently own, and the detailed analysis process we went through.

### Edmonton, Alberta Duplex

In October 2006, I purchased and closed on a side-by-side duplex. In addition to the main floor living areas, one side had a fully separate basement suite; the other had a partially finished basement suite. This offered the potential for renting out a total of four units.

Our strategy with this property was a long-term buy and hold. We also intended to increase our monthly rental income by investing money to finish the second basement suite. The market in Alberta at this time was doing quite well and still on the upswing, so we wanted to include Alberta property in our portfolio.

In this case, we went in with the understanding that this property would initially have negative cash flow, but completing the second basement suite would turn it into an investment with positive cash flow. In hindsight, I think I could have done better through purchasing property that has positive cash flow right from the start. However, as with anything, you can learn from your mistakes.

With regard to the mortgage, the seller was willing to hold a vendor take-back (VTB) at 15% of the purchase price and asked for 7% interest. This allowed us to acquire the property with a lot less money down. As usual, we hired a local property management company to take care of our new investment.

We could have acquired this property without the VTB, but chose to take advantage of the additional leverage. We had clients lined up who needed to borrow funds. Rather than putting it into our new property, we loaned this money ($60,600) to them. We offered them a second mortgage at 10.5% for a period of one year. They accepted these terms; by

taking advantage of the VTB, and then lending the original funds to one of our clients, we were able to benefit from the 3.5% spread.

The first table shows the basic income and expenses for the property, including debt service. The bottom line is the actual negative cash flow we originally carried, due partly to the fact that we had additional interest payments on the VTB. Without those payments, this property could have carried itself.

The second table shows our initial estimates of ROI. We estimated an appreciation rate of 5% per year over five years. The other factors in our calculation of ROI are total cash flow and mortgage principal reduction over the five-year period. This gave us an estimated ROI of approximately 64% per year. The ROI on this property was greater than in the next example because of the leverage we used by having the VTB.

The third table shows how the property has performed to date. Everything else being constant, we plugged in the value based on an appraisal we had done in the following year. With this updated variable, our ROI is approximately 52% per year. It decreased because we paid out the vendor take-back at the end of the first year.

*(See financial statements on page 92-93)*

## Ontario Townhouse

In August 2005, I closed on the purchase of a three-bedroom, 1.5 bath, end-unit townhome in a new subdivision in Milton, Ontario. This was a brand new, single-family home and our original agreement of purchase and sale with the builder was signed a year prior to closing.

Below are details about our area and property analysis that illustrate the depth of our inquiry and the amount of information that can be unearthed. We chose to invest in this town for several very good reasons. It showed clear signs of future growth, ongoing investment by both developers and

## Side By Side Duplex with One Complete Basement Suite

### TABLE ONE:
### BASIC INCOME AND EXPENSES

| | |
|---|---|
| Purchase price | $404,000.00 |
| Vendor take back (15% of purchase price) | $60,600.00 |
| Down payment | $40,400.00 |
| Closing costs | $3,000.00 |
| Total cash to close | $43,400.00 |
| Mortgage amount | $300,000.00 |
| **Monthly mortgage payments** | **$1,713.00** |

| Incoming Rent | Annual | Monthly |
|---|---|---|
| Unit one | $15,000.00 | **$1,250.00** |
| Unit two, upper | $12,000.00 | **$1,000.00** |
| Unit two, lower | $9,600.00 | **$800.00** |
| Assume 5% vacancy rate | $1,350.00 | $112.50 |
| Total rental income | $25,650.00 | $2,137.50 |

| Operating Expenses | Annual | Monthly |
|---|---|---|
| Property insurance | $1,440.00 | **$120.00** |
| Property taxes, 2007 | $4,800.00 | **$400.00** |
| Property management fees (5%) | $1,282.50 | **$106.88** |
| Repairs and maintenance | $1,200.00 | **$100.00** |
| Utilities (paid by tenant) | $ - | **$ -** |
| Condo fee (if applicable) | $ - | **$ -** |
| Super | $ - | **$ -** |
| Total operating expenses | $8,722.50 | $726.88 |
| **Net operating income** | **$16,927.50** | **$1,410.63** |

| Debt service | Annual | Monthly |
|---|---|---|
| Monthly mortgage payments | $20,556.00 | $1,713.00 |
| VTB | $4,242.00 | $353.50 |
| Total | $20,556.00 | $1,713.00 |
| **Cash flow** | **($3,628.50)** | **($302.38)** |

### TABLE TWO: PROFITABILITY BASED
### ON OUR ORIGINAL ASSUMPTIONS

*Projected Profit at End of Holding Period*

| | |
|---|---|
| Appreciation rate | 5% |
| Original purchase price | $404,000.00 |
| Year one | $424,200.00 |
| Year two | $445,410.00 |
| Year three | $467,680.50 |
| Year four | $491,064.53 |
| Year five | $515,617.75 |
| *Total equity growth over five years* | *$111,617.75* |
| Monthly cash flow over 5 years | $(18,142.50) |
| Mortgage principal pay-down over five years | $36,147.00 |
| *Total profit at end of 5 years* | *$129,622.25* |

**Initial Investment**

| | |
|---|---|
| Down payment | $ 40,400.00 |
| Additional funds invested | $ - |
| Total investment | $ 40,400.00 |

| | |
|---|---|
| *ROI over 5 years* | *321%* |
| *Average ROI per year* | *64%* |

## Side By Side Duplex with One Complete Basement Suite

### TABLE THREE: PROFITABILITY BASED ON ACTUAL PERFORMANCE

*Based on Appraisal of October, 2007*

| | |
|---|---|
| Original Purchase Price | $404,000.00 |
| Year 1 - based on appraisal | $550,000.00 |
| Year 2 - current estimated market value | $560,000.00 |
| Year 3 - assume 5% going forward | $588,000.00 |
| Year 4 | $617,400.00 |
| Year 5 | $648,270.00 |
| Total Equity Growth over 5 years | $244,270.00 |
| Monthly cash flow over 5 years | $(18,142.50) |
| Mortage - Principal pay-down over 5 years | $36,147.00 |
| *Total Profit at end of 5 years* | *$262,274.50* |

### Initial Investment

*VTB paid out at end of year 1*

| | |
|---|---|
| Down payment | $40,400.00 |
| Additional funds invested | $60,600.00 |
| Total investment | $101,000.00 |

| | |
|---|---|
| *ROI over 5 years* | *260%* |
| *Average ROI per year* | *52%* |

*Notes:*

- Potential for increasing income by finishing 2nd basement unit

- VTB allowed us to get in with less cash up front

- Funds that would have been used as a down payment were invested in a second mortgage at 10.5% so the interest we were earning more than offset the cost of taking the VTB for a one-year period

- We borrowed $60,600 in the form of a VTB at 7% per annum - $4,242 per year in interest

- Since we didn't have to use our $60,600 to close on the property we chose to lend it out to one of our clients in the form of a second mortgage at a rate of 10.5% per annum for a period of one year. By doing so we earned $6,363 in interest over that period

- The difference between the interest earned on our investment and the interest paid on the funds we borrowed was $2,121 which was additional income we received that year.

- Invested in a region with strong fundamentals for future growth.

businesses, and it was a favorable location for families.

Milton is strategically located along Highway 401, a major transportation route across southern Ontario, and Toronto Pearson International Airport is about a 30 minute drive to the east. This tactical location is favorable for attracting a diverse industry base. It also offers good transportation routes for people traveling through the area.

At the time we invested, its neighbor to the southeast, the town of Oakville, was expanding northward while the city of Mississauga, to the east, was expanding westward. Increasing prices in these larger communities, as well as the ease of access into Milton, made it an attractive relocation option for families. They could get more house for their money and still have a reasonable commute into the larger surrounding communities.

With this property, we used a long-term buy-and-hold strategy. We wanted to increase our asset base with the hope that, as we paid down the mortgage on the property, we would ultimately enjoy additional monthly income to support our lifestyle.

The key factor was ensuring that we received enough rental income to cover all property expenses as well as the debt service from the mortgage. After doing our due diligence on the location, our property analysis showed that there was sufficient projected cash flow for this property to satisfy our goals. After we had put down 25% of our own cash to close the deal, we set up a reserve fund to cover the cost of potential vacancies, future repairs, and maintenance.

As usual, we chose to use a local property manager to oversee our investment and included their fee in our expenses. Because we lived within an hour of the location, we considered self-managing the property, but concluded that our time was better spent in researching and securing other investment properties to grow our portfolio.

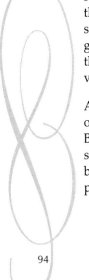

As with the previous example, the first table below outlines the basic income and expenses as well as our debt service. The bottom line is the actual, positive cash flow from this property on a monthly basis. Although it may seem small, over a growing portfolio the monthly cash flow starts to add up. In terms of vacancy, we are fortunate that our property manager has put excellent tenants in place, who treat the property well, and is proactive in ensuring that it stays tenanted. To date, we have experienced two or three months of vacancy on this property.

The second table shows our initial estimates of ROI. We estimated an appreciation rate of 5% per year over five years. The other factors in our calculation of ROI are total cash flow and mortgage principal reduction over the five year period. This gave us an estimated ROI of approximately 33% per year.

The third table shows how the property is performing to date. Everything else being constant, we are able to use the current market value derived from the sale of comparable homes in the area. With this updated variable, our ROI is approximately 49% per year.

# Single-Family Ontario Townhome

## TABLE ONE:
### BASIC INCOME AND EXPENSES

| | |
|---|---|
| Purchase price | $221,000.00 |
| Down payment (assuming 25%) | $55,250.00 |
| Closing costs | $2,000.00 |
| **Assignment Fee?** | |
| Total cash to close | $57,250.00 |
| Mortgage amount | $165,750.00 |
| **Monthly mortgage payments** | **$903.00** |

| Incoming Rent | Annual | Monthly |
|---|---|---|
| Unit 1 | $16,800.00 | $1,400.00 |
| Unit 2 | $ - | $ - |
| Assume 3% vacancy rate | $504.00 | $42.00 |
| Total rental income | $16,296.00 | $1,358.00 |

| Operating Expenses | Annual | Monthly |
|---|---|---|
| Property insurance | $420.00 | $35.00 |
| Property taxes, 2007 | $2,196.00 | $183.00 |
| Property management fees | $1,320.00 | $110.00 |
| Repairs and maintenance | $240.00 | $20.00 |
| Advertising | $240.00 | $20.00 |
| Condo fee (if applicable) | $ - | $ - |
| Other | $ - | $ - |
| Total operating expenses | $4,416.00 | $368.00 |

| Net Operating Income | | |
|---|---|---|
| | $11,880.00 | $990.00 |

| Debt Service | Annual | Monthly |
|---|---|---|
| Monthly mortgage payments | $10,836.00 | $903.00 |
| Total | $10,836.00 | $903.00 |
| **Cash Flow** | **$1,044.00** | **$87.00** |

## TABLE TWO: PROFITABILITY BASED ON OUR ORIGINAL ASSUMPTIONS

*Projected Profit at End of Holding Period*

| | |
|---|---|
| Appreciation rate | 5% |
| Original purchase price | $221,000.00 |
| Year one | $232,050.00 |
| Year two | $243,652.50 |
| Year three | $255,835.13 |
| Year four | $268,626.88 |
| Year five | $282,058.23 |
| *Total equity growth over five years* | *$61,058.23* |
| Monthly cash flow over 5 years | $5,220.00 |
| Mortgage principal pay-down over five years | $25,402.13 |
| *Total profit at end of 5 years* | *$91,680.36* |

**Initial Investment**

| | |
|---|---|
| Down payment | $ 55,250.00 |
| Total investment | $ 55,250.00 |

| | |
|---|---|
| *ROI over 5 years* | *166%* |
| *Average ROI per year* | *33%* |

## Side By Side Duplex with One Complete Basement Suite

**TABLE THREE: PROFITABILITY**
**BASED ON ACTUAL PERFORMANCE**

*Based on Current Market Value, August, 2008*

| | |
|---|---:|
| Original purchase price | $221,000.00 |
| Year one | $ - |
| Year two | $ - |
| Year three | $295,000.00 |
| Year four | $309,750.00 |
| Year five | $325,237.50 |
| *Total equity growth over five years* | *$104,237.50* |
| Monthly cash flow over 5 years | $5,220.00 |
| Mortgage principal pay-down over five years | $25,402.13 |
| *Total profit at end of 5 years* | *$134,859.63* |

**Initial Investment**

| | |
|---|---:|
| Down payment | $ 55,250.00 |
| Total investment | $ 55,250.00 |

| | |
|---|---:|
| *ROI over 5 years* | **244%** |
| *Average ROI per year* | **49%** |

## Doing a Repair-Cost Plan

Whether you are purchasing an investment property as a long-term hold or a short-term fix-and-flip, it is important to develop a repair-cost plan. Many people only take this into account when looking at fix-and-flip opportunities. However, having a repair-cost plan for a long-term hold allows you to carefully budget for these expenses through a conservative reserve fund.

A repair-cost plan is essentially a summary of the work—the needed repairs and optional renovations—that you are considering for a property and the projected cost of doing so. Developing an accurate estimate before you make an offer to purchase a property is essential. Your decision to proceed with a purchase will depend on these costs. (See Chapter Seven for more information about waiving conditions on an Agreement of Purchase and Sale.)

To develop your plan, you need a good relationship with several qualified contractors who can walk through a potential property and give you accurate estimates on the cost to repair or renovate it. If you have any intention of proceeding with a specific job, be sure to get a quote in writing. The last thing you want is getting a verbal estimate and then being surprised when you receive a much higher written estimate. Prepare a separate costing for each repair or improvement being considered.

As an investor, it is important to focus on making only those improvements that can significantly add value to your property. We recommend taking the time to calculate your return on anything you plan to do. You can ask your team of professionals to assist you with this, or do some of your own research online. For example, the Appraisal Institute of Canada has an interactive, Web-based calculator called RENOVA that can give you an estimate of the average payback for common renovations. RENOVA can be found at www.aiccanada.ca.

When you go through a potential investment, we also recommend working with a checklist so you won't forget any concerns about its condition. Fill out a checklist for every property you view. When looking at several properties, it is easy to get confused about which repairs or improvements were needed at each one. Also, bring a camera to take pictures of the property and the areas that require work. Put all this documentation into your property file.

Your checklist needs to be very detailed. Start compiling your checklist with resources that are already available rather than trying to create a new system from scratch. The Canada Mortgage and Housing Corporation provides a booklet called *Homebuying Step By Step*, in both printed and electronic formats, that contains several useful checklists. You can find it online at www.cmhc-schl.gc.ca.

## Leslie Comments on Regional Property Values

One of my lawyers once told me about a client who was excited about finding a small-town property at what they believed was an amazing price. It was a good-sized, all-brick, detached bungalow with three bedrooms, two bathrooms, and a two-car garage. The lot was oversized compared to what they were used to seeing and overall the property was in great shape. Best of all, it was offered for only $120,000!

Living in a large, metropolitan area, where an equivalent property would cost roughly twice this amount, the client thought they had found a great deal. After it was assessed, guess what the property was worth? That's right: exactly $120,000 and not a penny more. This investor was comparing apples to oranges: the prices and features of homes that were located within very different communities.

In addition, the property was located in a smaller town where the unemployment rate was much higher, the region was dependent on one major employer, and the vacancy rate was well above the national average. With nothing going on in the town and no major growth or infrastructure changes planned in the foreseeable future, the value of this investment would not have increased very much. Also, finding and retaining a suitable tenant would have proven very difficult.

The point is that you can't get caught up in the price or features of a property without considering where it is located. It is very important to look at what comparable properties are selling for. Also, as we discussed in the previous chapter, it is also important to do a careful study of what is happening in the area where you are considering investing.

Although this client could have picked up that property for a fraction of what a similar home would be worth in their own community, it would not have been much of a deal. Neither would this opportunity have contributed very much in terms of building the client's wealth.

WWW.R3BOOK.COM

# Chapter Seven

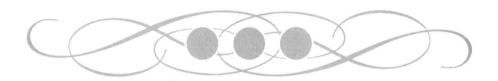

## *Closing the Deal:*

### ASTUTE FINANCING AND JOINT VENTURES

In the last two chapters of *R3: Real People with Real Strategies for Real Estate Investing*, we discussed how identifying promising communities and worthwhile investment properties both require careful planning to produce a winning outcome. The same approach is needed for successfully closing a real estate deal. There are clear steps involved in the process of making an offer to purchase, obtaining financing, and closing the deal on your new investment. This chapter outlines these steps, along with plenty of tips that will help the process happen more smoothly and productively for you.

### The Agreement of Purchase and Sale

After you have found the property you want to purchase, you present the seller with your terms by preparing an Agreement of Purchase and Sale, which is also known as an Offer to Purchase. For such a substantial investment, it would be wise to work with both your realtor and real estate lawyer in preparing your offer. (You should also sign a buyer-agency agreement with your realtor prior to this step.)

The Agreement of Purchase and Sale is a legal contract by which one party agrees to sell, and another agrees to purchase, a property. When finalized, it binds both parties to its terms. The details may vary for each country. This book offers Canadian examples of an international process that gets results, and below is a general description. Your real estate professional or legal counsel will know the specifics for the region in which you are planning to purchase property.

Although the Agreement of Purchase and Sale is legally binding for both parties when finalized, the strategic insertion of contingency clauses provides the option of canceling the contract should you discover something that would make the deal unacceptable. These are conditions attached to the offer that must be met to make the agreement binding to the buyer. Never submit an offer to purchase without including at least one contingency clause because it will ensure that you are not locked into buying a property if you discover that it does not satisfy your goals.

Contingency clauses are designed for your protection. It is rarely possible for you to have all of your facts assembled before your make an offer to purchase. With the use of the clauses outlined below, you can finalize details as an ongoing part of the process and then remove the conditions by signing a waiver that cancels them.

The process of making an offer to the seller, receiving a counteroffer, and then revising it again and again is very common. These negotiations can seem endless but are all part of the strategy involved in making the deal work for the buyer and the seller. Just remember that the Agreement of Purchase and Sale is a legal document and should be carefully prepared to ensure that you are protected throughout the negotiation process.

### Waiving a Contingency Clause

An offer can include both "subject to" and "right to" clauses. The first involves contingencies that can nullify a deal if not met, and the second are conditions that offer the buyer certain rights, such as access to the property for things such as renovations prior to owning it.

An offer that contains "subject to" clauses is called a conditional offer. The most common conditions included in offers are subject to financing, which allows buyers time to finalize their mortgage details; subject to inspection, which allows an accredited inspector to assess the condition of the property; and subject to appraisal, which determines the value of the property. As these contingency clauses are met, your agent will have you sign a document called a waiver to remove your condition. These conditions must be removed within the agreed-upon time period for the sale to become firm or legally binding. If, after the waiver is signed, the buyer decides to back out of the deal, he or she will lose the deposit and face legal action.

These contingency clauses provide a safe way for the buyer to back out of a deal without losing the deposit that must always accompany an offer. If the buyer is unable to obtain satisfactory mortgage financing, is not satisfied with the findings in the inspection report, or an appraisal determines the offering price is above the property's fair market value, the act of not waiving these clauses means that the offer becomes null and void and the buyer's deposit will be returned in full.

The following are descriptions of the common clauses that will be found in an Agreement of Purchase and Sale.

*Subject to financing.* The subject to financing clause allows the buyer to make an offer to purchase property before knowing what financing terms he or she is able to obtain. By using this clause, the buyer is assured that, if appropriate financing is not obtainable, the offer may be legally withdrawn and the deposit will be returned.

*Subject to inspection.* The subject to inspection clause makes the offer to purchase conditional upon the findings of an accredited property inspector. Once an inspection report is provided, it may allow the buyer to change the terms of the offer if a serious defect is uncovered by a professional inspection. It may also allow the buyer to legally back out of the deal and have the deposit returned. The buyer is typically required to pay for the inspection, but if defects are discovered it is money well spent.

*Subject to appraisal.* The subject to appraisal clause makes the offer conditional upon the results of a certified appraiser's analysis. A detailed report is provided to the buyer. If the reported value of the property is equal to or greater than the offer price, the condition can be removed. If the appraised value in the report is below the offered price, the buyer can legally withdraw the offer and the deposit will be returned.

*Right to assign.* The right to assign clause is primarily for the use of investors and can be enacted at any time prior to the closing date. This clause can be used to transfer the contractual rights and obligations from one party to another. This process often includes a payment for the transferred rights. Once the Agreement of Purchase and Sale has been assigned to a third party, the original purchaser is removed from all liability.

*Right to show.* The right to show clause can be used at any time prior to the closing date. This clause allows you to show the property to any interested third party by providing 48 hours notice to the seller. For example, if you are purchasing the property as a rental investment, the right to show clause allows you to acquire tenants prior to closing the deal.

In addition, the right to show and right to assign clauses can work together. You can show the property to a potentially interested third party, and then assign to them the original offer if they decide to take over your Agreement of Purchase and Sale.

**Financing Finesse**

The complex process involved in obtaining financing is of primary importance to any real estate investor. You can grow your portfolio exponentially by mastering some winning strategies for acquiring the funds you need. Developing these powerful skills is an ongoing process. It starts with careful planning and shrewd networking.

Begin by developing a strong and straightforward relationship with a carefully selected mortgage broker/lender. You should do this whether you need a mortgage at the moment or not. A solid, ongoing relationship with this professional puts you in a better position to obtain the financing you need when the right opportunity presents itself. At the same time, listen carefully to other sophisticated investors and learn what strategies they utilize to create wealth through real estate investing.

*Learn to leverage.* Most investors will buy real estate using leverage. As we discussed in Chapter Three, using leverage to acquire profitable investment opportunities is one of the biggest advantages of investing in real estate. But this strategy, which depends mainly on lender financing and only a small amount of your own money, must be used wisely. As top investment mogul Warren Buffet says, "When you combine ignorance and leverage, you get some pretty interesting results."

Keep in mind that there will always be risks involved. Work closely with your accountant to evaluate those risks, and review your strategy with your real estate lawyer. When analyzing opportunities, make sure that the rental income you can expect from the prospective investment will be sufficient to cover all related expenses plus the debt service. In addition, since it is inevitable that you will experience occasional rental vacancies, make sure that you have factored in an adequate reserve fund to cover these payments.

*Team up with other investors.* Another effective financing strategy is creating joint ventures where two or more parties combine their assets and expertise to achieve a profitable, successful real estate deal. This shrewd, sophisticated tactic is discussed in detail later in this chapter.

## Becoming an Ideal Mortgage Candidate

When you begin investing in real estate, it is a good idea to meet with your mortgage broker or lender very early in the process, and in person, to outline your plans. This will help you to develop a mutually beneficial relationship from the start. During your initial meetings, you will want to prove that you are a serious investor who is diligent about the kind of planning that accomplishes your goal.

Even though you may not have a specific opportunity in mind, it will familiarize your lender with what you are trying to accomplish. In turn, you will receive the benefit of knowing where you stand financially so that you will be confident about taking action when you locate your first opportunity.

Ask your lender to review your current financial situation and eligibility for a mortgage. Your lender will let you know how much financing you can obtain or will even pre-approve a mortgage for you. This will include obtaining a copy of your credit report and offering feedback about anything that you should correct or improve.

If you have any outstanding financial obstacles, it would be wise to address them immediately. Proactively fix any problems in your credit rating so that you are well positioned

as a candidate for a mortgage prior to needing one. By resolving any problems, you can also improve your credit rating and the amount of money you qualify for.

Keep in mind that, should you identify issues that make you ineligible for a mortgage, you can still begin investing in real estate while you work on cleaning up your finances. To do so, you will have to use other people's money or credit. One way to do this is by working with other investors on a joint venture, and contributing the time and energy required to get the detail work done.

### Credit-worthy character traits

The way you present yourself to a lender is also essential. Although the property is of interest to the lender, the quality of the mortgage application is very important, especially during times when lending conditions are tightened. Lenders look at several variables in determining whether or not to approve your mortgage application. The most basic of these is often referred to as the "five Cs of credit."

*Character:* When meeting a lender in person, they will look at how you present yourself (i.e., the type of person you are). First impressions will be very important, so be sure to present yourself as a professional, organized, and diligent investor. In many cases, you won't actually meet the person who will be financing your mortgage. You will be working with the lender's agent, and factors such as your employment history and education will help to depict the type of person you are. As we discuss below, by developing a clear and concise presentation format, you will demonstrate that you are organized and on top of your financial situation.

*Collateral:* This is usually the property that you are purchasing. The lender's mortgage is secured against the property. Should you fail to meet the obligations of the mortgage, your lender can foreclose on the property and recover the loan. This is why lenders require an appraisal. They have to be certain that the value of the property is accurate and sufficient to cover the loan should anything go wrong. For more information, see the section below about appraisers.

*Capital:* As a real estate investor, this refers to the amount of your down payment. The lender has certain requirements in terms of how much of your own money you must put into the deal.

*Credit:* The lender thoroughly reviews your credit history to ensure that you have been responsible with previous credit obligations. How you managed your credit in the past is a good indicator of how you will fulfill your obligations for the mortgage they may provide to you.

*Capacity:* This is your ability to make the payments on the mortgage. Below are two formulas that your lender will use in calculating your capacity to repay the loan.

GDS RATIO (Gross Debt Service Ratio): This calculation measures your ability to make payments on a mortgage. Divide the costs of paying the principal, interest, property taxes, secondary financing, heating, and condominium fees by your gross monthly income and then multiply by 100. Lenders usually like to see this ratio at 32% or less.

$$GDS = \frac{PITH \text{ (Principal, Interest, Property Taxes, Heat)}}{\text{Gross Annual Household Income}}$$

TDS RATIO (Total debt service ratio): This is a slightly more detailed analysis of your financial fitness. You divide all costs associated with your housing and other financial obligations, such as car loans and credit cards, by your gross monthly income. Lenders usually like to see this ratio at 40% or less.

$$TDS = \frac{PITH \text{ (Principal Interest, Property Taxes, Heat)} + \text{Payments on ALL debts}}{\text{Gross Annual Household Income}}$$

## The Mortgage Application

You are more likely to get your application looked at, and approved more quickly, if you present your lender will all the necessary documentation in a clear, straightforward, and appealing format. Take the time and effort to put together an organized and attractive financing binder. In our own ventures, we have found that this kind of carefully planned presentation has led to the greatest success. We now routinely include templates for a complete financing binder in our course because of the value it provides.

It is not just about the information you provide but also how it is presented, as this says a great deal about your professionalism and thorough dedication to your goals. Including all of the required information saves your lender a great deal of time. It is much more efficient than having to go back and forth because you are missing critical information, and a lender will remember this. By making it easy to do business together, things will be much more favorable for you the next time around. You will be seen as an organized investor who pays attention to detail.

Start compiling this information package for your first mortgage application, and then use it as a template that can be easily updated for future applications. If you plan to grow your portfolio, keeping this template up-to-date not only saves you time but it is also a good way to track how you are doing financially year after year.

It can be exhilarating and motivating to watch your assets increase as you add new properties to your portfolio. Equally heady is watching your liabilities decrease as your mortgages are paid down. This is part of having that all-important baseline so that you can gauge your performance and growth over time.

Things to include in your mortgage application package are:

- cover page with a photo of the property you are purchasing

- clear description of your plans (For example: "We wish to obtain financing for the purchase of a three-bedroom townhome located in Hamilton, Ontario. We are purchasing this as an investment property with a current (or projected) rental income of $1,300 per month. Our strategy is 'buy and hold' and we plan to keep this property for five years or more.")

- clear copy of the Agreement of Purchase and Sale (see Chapter Eight for more information)

- personal financial documents, such as a net worth/balance sheet and income statement

- your tax notice (In Canada, this is called a Notice of Assessment) for the past two years. This annual statement, sent by federal revenue authorities to taxpayers, details the amount of income tax owed. It includes the amount of their tax refund, any tax credits, and income tax already paid.)

- T4 slip or the equivalent in your country (A T4 slip is the Canadian tax form showing an employee's pay details. It is provided by the individual's employer and states the income paid to the employee as well as the taxes withheld.)

- current pay stubs

- employment or contract verification letter

- letter from your accountant confirming income

- summary of all investments and copies of recent statements

- summary of all credit and copies of recent statements

- summary of all your rental property (For each property, include the photo, address, year it was purchased, purchase price, current market value, current mortgage value, monthly mortgage payments, taxes, insurance, and rental income. Also include copies of financial statements and lease agreements for each property in your portfolio.)

- current credit report (You can obtain this yourself by contacting a credit-reporting company, such as Equifax in Canada or the U.S.)

- confirmation or verification of personal funds to be used in the down payment

At some point during the mortgage application process, the lender will request an appraisal of the property. You will usually be offered a list of approved appraisers. These professionals ensure that the value of the property is in line with the purchase price on your offer. As an investor, you should understand the appraisal process and how the value of property is determined.

### The Valuation of Real Estate

An appraisal is important because it gives both you and your lender a clear picture of the property's value. It helps both parties to make well-informed decisions regarding your prospective investment. The appraisal process provides you with a good basis for negotiating the price that is paid, and the result of an appraisal directly impacts the amount of mortgage that your lender ultimately approves.

Dr. William N. Kinnard, in his book *Income Property Valuation*, describes the process: "An appraisal is a professionally derived conclusion about the present worth or value of specified rights or interests in a particular parcel of real estate under stipulated market conditions or decision standards. Moreover, it is (or should be) based on the professional judgment and skill of a trained practitioner. Its conclusions should be presented in a thoroughly logical and convincing way to a client or an interested third party who requires the value estimate to help make a decision or solve a problem involving the real estate in question."

When a lender is in the process of determining the amount of a mortgage to offer you, he or she will send an appraiser to provide an estimate of the property's value. Often the cost of having the appraisal done is passed on to you as the buyer; if this is the case, you are entitled to receive a copy of the final appraisal report. As expressed in Dr. Kinnard's quote above, the standards for this report include a logical and convincing argument to support the conclusions reached regarding the fair market value of the property.

When the appraised value of a property comes in lower than the purchase price, the lender will usually offer you a percentage of the appraised value and not the higher amount that you requested. The following is an example of how you will be affected when an appraisal comes in lower than the price you negotiated in your Agreement of Purchase and Sale.

Assuming that you will be providing a 25% down payment, you applied for a mortgage using the following financing structure:

| | |
|---|---|
| Purchase Price: | $200,000 |
| Appraised Value: | $200,000 or higher |
| Maximum Mortgage: | $150,000 |
| Down Payment: | $ 50,000 |

However, the appraised value came in lower than the value of your Offer to Purchase. This results in the following adjustment:

| | |
|---|---|
| Purchase Price: | $200,000 |
| Appraised Value: | $180,000 |
| Maximum Mortgage: | $135,000 |
| Down Payment: | $ 65,000 |

In this example, you now have to come up with another $15,000 for your down payment. The good news is that, if you make your offer *subject to appraisal*, as we discussed, you don't have to be stuck with making up the difference between your offered price and the appraised value. You can either renegotiate the price of the property with the seller or you can back out of the deal entirely with no financial consequences except the cost of the appraisal.

Depending on the structure you have put in place to handle your real estate investments, you may be able to write off the cost of doing the appraisal. You should consult your accountant with regards to the eligibility of this write-off.

If you feel that the appraiser has, for some reason, undervalued the property, you can ask the lender to re-examine the appraisal. Assuming that you have received full documentation with a clear argument to support the appraisal, you can review this and provide your reasons for believing that the property was undervalued.

### The Three Most Common Appraisal Methods

Described below are the three methods currently available for calculating a property's value. Appraisals of properties that are typically purchased by investors may give greater weight to the income capitalization method. It is important to note that, when there is insufficient financial data for similar properties in a given market, appraisers may use all three appraisal approaches.

*Direct cost or replacement cost method*: This entails estimating the current cost to reconstruct or reproduce the property, including all improvements at the date of the appraisal, less depreciation. The value of the land is then added to this figure.

*Direct comparison or sales comparison method:* This is the most commonly used method. With this approach, an appraiser would look at recent sales of properties of similar size, quality, and location to determine the market value of the property being analyzed. The rationale is that the price paid for recent sales is indicative of what buyers are willing to pay and is a good reflection of fair market value.

*Income capitalization method:* This method is generally used for properties that generate income. The present value of a property is directly related to its net operating income or projected net operating income.

By understanding the various methods and fundamentals behind the valuation of property, a sophisticated investor can make informed, educated, and solid investment decisions. This is especially helpful when entering into new regions because it allows you to understand local market values. Remember, it is not so much the price of a property that is important but rather what that price is relative to similar properties in that region.

## Leslie's Advice on Mortgage Financing

Before you waive the *subject to financing* condition on your offer, be sure to have a mortgage commitment letter in your hands. You may get a verbal approval on your mortgage application, or your lender may be certain that you will get approved and say so. But this does not constitute a firm contract to provide a mortgage for your investment; you should never remove the financing condition without having your confirmation in writing.

In most cases, your lender's prediction will be accurate, and your financing will then progress smoothly. But you do not want to put yourself in a situation where you waive your financing condition prematurely and then are unable to secure the appropriate financing for the deal.

I have been in situations where I have not been able to get a mortgage commitment letter prior to my financing condition expiring. In one situation with a commercial property, things were delayed because the appraisal took longer than expected. Because I did not have definite confirmation of my financing, I was unable to waive this condition.

I wrote a letter to the seller explaining my situation and requested their approval in extending my conditional period for financing. As long as you have a valid reason for requiring an extension, the seller will usually work with you.

### Closing the Deal

The final few days before your closing can be a very busy, emotional, and exciting period for both the buyer and seller. Closing on a property means the sale is complete and all the terms and conditions of the purchase agreement have been met. Once the sales contract and loan commitment are signed, both the buyer and seller are obligated to complete the transaction. For the buyer, failure to do so will cause the deposit to be forfeited. For both parties, backing out of the contract can mean facing a possible lawsuit.

Closing is the point where the title search is completed, the mortgage funds are ready to be disbursed, and the paperwork on the purchase is ready to be signed and recorded. Once all documents have been signed, funds disbursed, and the deed and mortgage have been recorded, the transaction has been closed. In most cases, the property is then legally yours.

The closing date is set during negotiation of the Agreement of Purchase and Sale, and will usually be many weeks after the buyer's offer is formally accepted by the seller. On this day, before you can take legal possession of your investment property, you will have to visit your lawyer's office to sign all of the closing documents that are part of finalizing the sale.

Your lender will forward the mortgage money to your lawyer and you will produce the balance of the purchase price, along with the closing costs. (Your lawyer will provide you with a statement of adjustments that indicates how much you need to bring with you, usually in the form of a certified check or money order.) Your lawyer will forward these proceeds from the sale to the vendor's lawyer, then register the home in your name and provide you with a deed and the keys to your new home.

### The Escrow Account

You will hear the term "escrow" during this process. Escrow is where a third party holds money or property in trust for another party until certain conditions are met. An example is the deposit money given to your real estate agent to accompany your offer on a property. That money goes into an escrow account until you close. Your lawyer also holds your down payment and the money from your lender in an escrow account until all the closing details are finalized. You may also keep your money in escrow with your mortgage company.

### Why You Need Title Insurance

Title insurance protects property owners and their lender against fraudulent activities or claims and liens on the property. This insurance also protects you from the effects of an incorrect appraisal as well as property line disputes and unidentified easements. (An easement is when a third party, such as a utility company, is legally allowed access to your property; a survey should clearly state if and where an easement may be located.)

Your lender may require title insurance before releasing the funds for your mortgage. We believe that buying this insurance is a very good idea. When purchasing a property, it effectively guarantees that the property is yours and goes further than the property's deed in ensuring this. Title insurance is a policy that you pay only once, typically on the closing date. The policy covers the amount you purchased the property for, so when your property increases in value the policy's coverage will not. However, the policy lasts until you sell the property.

## Closing Costs

These are costs that you must pay in addition to the purchase price of your investment. Examples of closing costs are described below.

*Legal fees:* These are for preparing and recording the required documents. In real estate transactions, there are usually two lawyers involved (one for the buyer and one for the seller) to ensure that both parties receive fair representation. These fees are normally paid by the respective parties.

*Title fees:* These costs are for title searches and title insurance, and are normally paid by the seller. If your lawyer conducts these searches, they will be added to your legal fees.

*Survey fees:* These are necessary for commercial properties. The land survey verifies the property's dimensions and lot size.

*Application fees:* These government fees are charged when transferring the ownership of a property. The buyer's loan application will also include an administrative fee, which is owed to the lender.

*Commission fees:* Normally one of the highest closing costs, the real estate agent is paid through a commission fee.

*Land transfer tax:* Where applicable, it is a tax applied to the purchase price of a property as part of the transfer of ownership.

Closing costs are often negotiated between the buyer and seller during the process of finalizing an offer. For example, there may be fees that the seller will agree to pay, such as the cost of a property inspection. All closing costs are payable on closing day and can range from 1.5% to 4% of the property's selling price.

### Closing Date

The closing date is when the buyer's lawyer will file the deed with the government, finalizing the transfer of ownership. This is also the date when the buyer's mortgage begins. The sale of the property becomes final and the new owner takes possession.

With commercial investments, the closing date can be many months after the buyer and seller have finalized the Agreement of Purchase and Sale. It can be a key point in the negotiations between the seller and buyer to purchase the property. For example, depending on the seller's financial situation, he or she will either want to close before their current fiscal year end or push the closing date into the following fiscal year. As a buyer, if you have flexibility and can accommodate the seller's requested closing date, you may be able to push them to give in on some of the terms that are more important to you.

### Deed

This is the legal document signed by both the vendor and purchaser, which transfers the ownership of a property. This document will be registered with the government on the closing date and constitutes legal evidence of ownership.

### Profiting with Joint Ventures

In real estate, you will find that many sophisticated investors participate in joint ventures. Combining resources is the essence of what a joint venture is all about. There is always strength in numbers, and in a real estate venture this can bring out the best of both parties, resulting in the creation of a winning, profitable investment. Usually, one partner is the real estate expert; the other is the money partner, providing the cash to close and sometimes contributing his or her credit worthiness to obtain financing on a property. In large deals, there may be more partners involved.

A well-structured joint venture can be very beneficial to all parties. When selecting a potential partner, you must take into account that person's attitude, professionalism, decision-making process (or inability to make a decision), and mindset for success. Look for complementary skills and always assess whether your potential partner has a logical, business-oriented attitude.

You will need to create a formal structure to govern your relationships within the venture. Consider issues such as how voting will occur to make decisions and who will have the day-to-day operational control. Another consideration will be a clearly defined structure for splitting profits, based on such factors as money invested, time and labor spent in fixing up properties, and time spent in management of the venture.

Even before you enter into your business relationship, your planning should also include a clear mechanism for exiting the joint venture. If it should fail, or the relationship between the members falls apart, everyone needs to receive their fair share of the venture. The terms of this "economic divorce" must be clearly specified, including how to buy out a member (or paying the beneficiaries in the case of a death) and how to set the price for this buyout (such as using the net equity of a member's interest in the venture).

Always operate a joint venture through a protective legal entity such as a corporation or an LLC (limited-liability corporation). Avoid structuring your venture as a partnership, which makes all partners personally liable for the partnership's debts.

## Rick Describes His Best Joint-Venture Partnership

I have learned through the years that to be successful in business and in life you need to focus on your goals, be positive, and surround yourself with the right people. Working with others who share the same values, purpose, and interests can motivate, encourage, and inspire you to succeed. I never realized how true this was until I met and started working with Leslie.

Over the years, I have known many people who were a lot of talk but never acted on their investment ideas or achieved their objectives. Most of them focused on sounding big rather than on being big. Leslie proved to be different. I found her vision and determination very powerful and was inspired by her passion to accomplish the investing goals she set for herself. Her attitude was refreshing.

When developing a project or pursuing a new idea or strategy, Leslie works hard to ensure its success. It is motivating to know there are no limits to what can be accomplished when working with her. Her business knowledge and drive to achieve, as well as her ability to challenge others, brings out the best in my abilities. This synergy, and our shared passion for investing, enables us to attain great success in business, including our joint real estate ventures.

We have always recognized the value of joint ventures and will continue to do so as we grow our portfolios. Leslie and I have worked closely together on various joint-venture projects. These included a rental property in Kitchener, Ontario and the development of a lakefront property in Lowbanks, Ontario. Leslie had finalized many investment deals prior to meeting me and never hesitated to share what she learned along the way. She has also built a large network of quality people simply because she is as honest, caring, and helpful in business as she is in friendship.

By working with other investors in joint-venture opportunities, we all capitalize on the strengths of each party and have access to a larger pool of investment funds. We combine our investment expertise to effectively locate, negotiate, and acquire appropriate properties. As a group, we are able to move forward much faster than would be possible if we were to work alone.

Leslie and I are working on one of our latest and biggest projects, a condo conversion in Hamilton, Ontario. Together, we are overseeing and managing all of the intricate details of the project from start to finish. With larger projects such as this, it is necessary to have access to greater amounts of capital. Some of the funds to acquire and renovate the property are coming from a lender in the form of a mortgage; the balance of the money is being raised by working with other investors. Without joint-venture partners, a project like this would be difficult to undertake.

Although a condo conversion seems like a fairly simple process, in reality it is a complex project requiring a skilled group of professionals to implement a solid, detailed plan. We are jointly building the team of experts we need to ensure a successful and profitable venture, both for ourselves and our investor colleagues. The team that oversees this type of project must be accountable, detail-oriented, focused, and forward thinking.

Along with our joint-venture projects, Leslie and I have worked together on investment deals for our own individual companies. Recently, I helped Leslie to purchase a 30,000-square-foot office building in Hamilton, Ont. In addition to being a successful investment and providing rental income, it is also the new location of our corporate offices.

Leslie has not only become my biggest supporter and inspiration to succeed, she is one of my closest friends. I find that we have a great deal of confidence in ourselves and in each other. We are a very powerful team; we challenge each other's ideas and push each other to do well. I look forward to a long and successful future working with Leslie, helping each other to stay focused and inspiring our determination to achieve all our investment goals.

**Leslie Partners with a Friend to Grow Her Portfolio**

One of the most common obstacles for investors is the lack of sufficient down payment funds and the inability to obtain financing. While planning how to grow my portfolio, I quickly realized that this was also going to be a challenge for me. On paper, my net worth was increasing, but, as many investors discover, this doesn't necessarily translate into income or cash flow in the short term.

Because my philosophy has always been to create long-term, sustainable wealth, I wasn't doing fix-and-flip deals or using other strategies that might have allowed me to capitalize on my investments sooner. I was in it for the long haul; I wanted to acquire solid property and hold onto it, so coming up with more money to acquire new properties became a challenge.

Fortunately, I had taken the time to network and build solid relationships with other sophisticated investors by joining organizations such as the Real Estate Investment Network in Canada. I also actively participated in several local investment groups. You can't underestimate the value of building relationships based on accountability, integrity, and diligence. Having these relationships in place allowed me to learn from more experienced investors and also gave me access to their resources.

I began learning about the value of joint ventures and how they could benefit all parties involved. Working with my best friend, Tanya Skaljac, we came up with a plan to pool our financial resources as well as our creditworthiness. Both of us had existing investments but we didn't have enough cash on hand to move into the new investments we had been looking at. In addition, we figured that a joint mortgage application would be much stronger and more favorable to our lenders.

The enthusiasm we felt as we acquired our next few properties was amazing. By combining our resources, we first acquired a multi-family complex together, and then each added another single-family townhome to our portfolios. The most important thing was that we shared common values, we had a common vision about the properties we were acquiring together, and we had a predefined exit strategy should either party have to pull out of the investment. By taking the time to discuss all the possible obstacles in advance, we built a partnership based on trust and respect.

Not only did we work toward acquiring property together, we also began hosting networking events and sending out newsletters to everyone on our power team as well as potential joint-venture candidates. By combining our passion for real estate and enthusiasm for running a business, we were able to increase our asset bases substantially in our first year.

As with anything else, once you begin to understand the fundamentals behind sound investing it can become an addiction. I began to realize how passionate I was becoming about real estate investing while Tanya and I were out for a drive. Somehow, no matter where we were going or what we were doing, we always ended up pulling over to look at properties for sale or driving through neighborhoods to look around. Day after day, most of our conversations ended up geared toward business, the real estate market, our existing properties, and what we could do to improve our performance. It was all encompassing; even with the challenges and obstacles placed in front of us, we never wavered.

Working with other investors who share your mindset can be one of the fastest ways to grow your portfolio. We all eventually hit a limit or ceiling, after which it becomes difficult to continue acquiring property alone. By thinking creatively, you will see this not as an obstacle but as an opportunity to work with others in creating a mutually beneficial relationship.

### A Family Affair

My family is an integral part of my life and it was important for me to share my knowledge and enthusiasm with them. Just

123

as my father shared his experiences, attitude, and knowledge with me, I began doing the same with my family, mainly through sharing in our wealth-creation meetings. But they will also be one of the first groups of people I turn to as potential joint-venture partners.

Most of my cousins who participate in our family wealth-creation meetings have expressed an interest in real estate investing. Some already own their own properties, while others have yet to grow into home ownership. Because of the diversity in their personal financial situations, investing in real estate isn't something that they could do individually at this point in their lives. So, as a family we decided to create a joint venture where everyone, regardless of where they were in their lives, could participate.

We thought it would be a great way for everyone to learn more about the process of real estate investing. It also allowed us to leverage our different strengths and financial capabilities. Those of us with more experience had the opportunity to teach the others. In addition, those without experience brought their own unique perspectives to the table. By pooling our resources, we became a strong team. We were each able to grow our asset base by acquiring a piece of solid, income-producing real estate.

We learned about a property through a group of associates in Fort Saskatchewan, Alberta. They specialize in the commercial real estate market and provide investment opportunities in the form of limited partnerships. This particular property was outside of their area of focus, so they offered to assign the contract to us. It was an up/down duplex located in a good area of Fort Saskatchewan. Vacant at the time, it had good potential for attracting quality tenants. After gathering and analyzing all of the necessary information, our due diligence showed that this was an excellent property to acquire as a family and hold for the long term.

Although it was a little more complex than other joint ventures, because there were multiple parties involved, we were able to structure it to benefit everyone. We also made sure to walk through the entire process together so that everyone involved fully understood the transaction. We put a strong joint-venture agreement into place and worked together to come up with a long-term management plan as well as an exit strategy.

The thrill of accomplishing this and learning to work together was an excellent experience for all of us and we still own this property today. We will likely hold onto it for the next few years and then reap the rewards of our efforts together.

Creating wealth and becoming successful is much more enjoyable if the ones you care most about are there to share in it with you. Currently, my immediate family has a residential real estate portfolio that consists of 27 properties throughout Ontario and Alberta. We are constantly striving to grow this by adding new properties to the portfolio when we come across solid, income-producing opportunities.

My dad always used to tell me that 50% of something is better than 100% of nothing. From a business perspective, what he meant was that partnering with someone to make a deal work, if done properly, is a much better option than having to walk away from a deal.

WWW.R3BOOK.COM

*Chapter Eight*

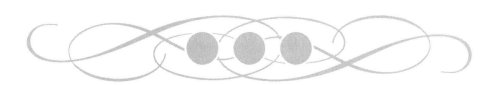

*Valuable Networking:*

BUILDING YOUR SUCCESS TEAM

It is often said that your net worth is directly proportional to the size of your network. Successful investors continuously grow their circle of real estate contacts because of the opportunities this brings, both to increase their skills and to learn about potential investment ventures.

Actively surround yourself with other investors and real estate professionals who can help you to build your portfolio and overcome obstacles. In developing these mutually beneficial relationships, you need to earn the respect you deserve as an astute investor. To start off right, you must be able to talk the talk.

As with any industry, the world of real estate investing includes a specialized vocabulary that you have to understand

and use effectively. Initially, it may feel awkward working with unfamiliar terms, but with time and experience they will become a natural part of your vocabulary. Educate yourself by reading business magazines, real estate magazines, newsletters, and other publications that can increase your knowledge of the terms and concepts you will be using during meetings with your team members, joint-venture partners, and fellow investors.

When you come across terms, phrases, or formulas that you don't understand, depending on the circumstance you can write things down and look them up later. You can also ask a trusted source within your network to clarify what they mean, and use this conversation as an opportunity to express your commitment to growing both your real estate portfolio and your network of contacts.

## Building Your Team

Your success is largely dependent on who you surround yourself with. To become a winning real estate investor, we recommend that you build strong relationships with other experienced investors and utilize these sources to identify the opportunities that will help you to develop a profitable portfolio. Read Rick's discussion at the end of this chapter for more tips on money-making networking.

In addition, as we discussed in previous chapters, the process involved in closing your real estate deals is a strategic and complex series of steps. Your success will benefit from the specialized skills of a carefully selected group of astute professionals. These skilled and shrewd realtors, lawyers, accountants, mortgage brokers, property inspectors, contractors, insurance agents, and appraisers will enhance your ability to secure profitable real estate transactions.

It is often said that you become the average of the people you spend the most time with. So be certain to surround yourself

with positive, motivating, experienced professionals that will constantly push and challenge you to achieve more and then sincerely celebrate your successes with you.

### Realtors

As we discussed in chapter six, we maintain contact with many different realtors, employing their skills to identify the types of property that we believe will offer investment potential. Realtors will bring to you information about properties for sale in their area, some of which may not be available to the public. Each realtor will offer different expertise and resources for you to draw on.

In the Kitchener-Waterloo and Cambridge areas of Ontario, we work with Leah Small and her team from Remax when buying or selling our investment properties. Leah has several years of experience with the area and also works with other investors. Having a realtor with experience working with investors is essential. They are more likely to understand that, although an investor may take more time to acquire their ideal property, the investor will likely be making multiple purchases in the future. In contrast, a client looking to purchase a home may require the services of a realtor only once or twice in their lifetime.

A realtor will provide you with specific details such as the number of units, bedrooms and bathrooms, building type, square footage, location, comparables, property taxes, and price. He or she will also be able to provide detailed market and rental statistics.

You will use your realtor's expertise and the market statistics to estimate what a potential property is worth and whether the seller is asking a price that is above or below the current average. Rental statistics will allow you to calculate whether this property will have a positive cash flow based on the rental income generated after all expenses. These statistics will be based on the neighborhood, type of property, square footage, and details such as the number of levels, bathrooms, bedrooms, or units.

A realtor will also help to gather essential information about income-producing property, such as expenses and revenues. For example, to purchase a commercial building you will need to know the price per unit, the asking price, and the average price per unit for comparable property in the area. The expense list will include hydro, water, maintenance, and the property manager's costs. The revenue list will include income from the lease/rental of the units, parking, signage, and miscellaneous income such as laundry and vending units. You will also need to know leasing details to calculate how you can increase the rents/leases on the units. This information will tell you if you will have a negative, net, or positive cash flow and how you could enhance it.

*Vendor Take-Back Mortgages*

A skilled realtor also knows about promising opportunities for arranging a vendor take-back mortgage (VTB), which is a second mortgage on the property that is held by the seller or vendor. Also known as a seller-financed deal, this is a well-known practice that can benefit both parties.

Many sellers who have a large amount of equity in their property will offer a VTB, holding back a percentage of the purchase price. The seller is repaid, with interest, over the agreed-upon term; if the buyer does not make these payments, it could result in losing the property to the seller. This is more commonly offered by owners of commercial property or investors unloading their portfolios.

Sellers receive tax benefits because they do not claim full capital gains; they still have money invested in the property. Buyers often receive an interest rate that is lower than market rates, and can acquire the property with less cash up front. It's a win-win for both parties, so always ask your realtor if the seller is willing to take a VTB.

Choosing realtors with plenty of experience is a very smart move. A seasoned realtor is better at negotiating a great deal for you while ensuring that all the steps, from making the offer to closing the deal, are completed correctly.

## The Lawyer

Before signing the contract to purchase a property, both the buyer and seller need to consult a lawyer to ensure that the transaction is done correctly and legally. Purchasing a property will probably be one of your largest financial transactions. A good real estate lawyer can protect your interests while resolving any potential legal issues you might encounter prior to signing the contract.

A good lawyer will also prepare and provide you with all closing documents for your purchases and sales, including a title search to ensure that there are no outstanding liens on the property. She or he will also prepare a statement of adjustments identifying the amount of money required to close on the property after all legal fees, disbursements, and adjustments between the buyer and seller are accounted for. Other duties will include transferring the deed or title from the seller's name into the buyer's name, acquiring the paperwork from the bank or mortgage company for the buyer to sign, and reviewing the contracts to ensure that all obligations are met by both parties.

The lawyer you choose must also be proficient in sheriff sales, which is the sale of a foreclosure property by a third party such as a bank or other mortgage company, and tax sales. Look for a lawyer experienced in VTB deals to advise you, confirming details such as how payments will be made (monthly, quarterly, or yearly), the interest rate, and other terms and conditions. A lawyer that understands these transactions is essential for real estate investing.

It is also important for your lawyer to have experience in dealing with the "cash-back-on-closing" concept. Getting cash back on closing is risky and, at times, illegal. For example, if the seller agrees to sell the property to the buyer for $250,000 while the appraised value is only $200,000, this creates $50,000 cash back at closing to the seller, which is considered fraud.

The lawyer you hire *must* have many years of experience in this business. You need a lawyer with experience to ensure that all steps and procedures are conducted with due diligence. A lawyer without proven skill and judgment in the purchasing and selling of real estate can create many financial problems for you down the road.

### The Accountant

It is essential to use a highly qualified, well-educated accountant in the field of real estate and its tax laws. This experienced professional can give you astute advice about the best way to structure your real estate business. Your accountant must be able to identify accounting and auditing problems related to every real estate transaction and find solutions that benefit you as their client.

A good accountant understands real estate tax credits, deductions, and tax break incentives, shrewdly guiding you in decisions concerning your portfolio. For example, consider the following discussion about the tax implications of selling a Canadian investment property.

*Capital Gains vs. Business Income*

Although most investors are in it for the long term, it often becomes necessary to supplement a growing portfolio with short-term investment strategies. These might include buying and flipping single houses or larger projects such as condo conversions. An experienced accountant can help you to plan for the relevant tax consequences.

When disposing of a property, the difference between having that income treated as capital gains versus business income can often influence whether a project is worth pursuing. In Canada, capital gains are taxed at a 50% inclusion rate, which means that 50% of the gain is added to your income for the year and taxed at your marginal tax rate. This is an obvious advantage over business income, of which 100% is taxed. In addition, if the Canada Revenue Agency decides that the

property being disposed of is "inventory," it may disallow the carrying costs incurred while renovating.

Canada's *Income Tax Act* does not clearly define the circumstances under which the gain from a real estate deal will be treated as income or capital. Instead, an "income tax interpretation" bulletin states that the courts will consider many different factors, such as:

- the taxpayer's intention with respect to the real estate at the time of its purchase

- feasibility of the taxpayer's intention

- extent to which this intention was carried out by the taxpayer

- evidence that the taxpayer's intention changed after purchase of the property

- geographical location and zoned use of the real estate when it was acquired

- the nature of the business, profession, calling, or trade of the taxpayer and any associates

- the extent to which borrowed money was used to finance the real estate acquisition and any terms of financing

- the length of time during which the real estate was held by the taxpayer

- the existence of persons other than the taxpayer who have an interest in the property

- the nature of the occupation of these other persons as well as their stated intentions and courses of conduct

- factors that motivated the sale of the property

- evidence that the taxpayer and/or associates dealt extensively in real estate

As you can see, the implications in tax laws can be very complex to interpret. We recommend working closely with your chartered accountant to analyze potential projects and the relevant tax consequences. Without careful planning, the differences in potential taxation will definitely affect your anticipated bottom line.

### The Mortgage Broker

Mortgage brokers are independent and deal with many different lenders, making their advice impartial with only your best interest in mind. This gives you more choices for arranging the best deal on your mortgages at competitive rates.

Mortgage brokers are willing to disclose details such as penalties for early mortgage payouts and can arrange 90% financing on first and second mortgages. There are many different types of mortgages available; your broker will help you determine the right mortgage to achieve your goals. In addition to banks and other financial institutions, brokers often develop strong professional relationships with private lenders who can offer a wide variety of less conventional mortgage products.

### The Inspector

In today's world of buying and selling real estate, no deal is truly finalized until the property inspection is complete. It is a condition that appears in most real estate offers. The result of that inspection can make or break a deal; the inspector is your agent for identifying structural or mechanical problems with a property.

Your property inspector must have at least five years in the business and you need to confirm their credibility. In addition, a qualified inspector should have at least $1 million of insurance for errors and omissions.

The property inspector will provide you with a detailed analysis of the condition of the property: what is in good working order, what needs repairs or replacement, and what will need attention in the future. A property inspection will include items such as the foundation, roof, doors, windows, and exterior surfaces; the electrical, plumbing, heating, and air conditioning; driveways, sidewalks, and patios; garages; and septic tanks.

If you are serious about buying or selling property, develop a great working relationship with an experienced, well-qualified inspector who can save you both money and hassles. This professional will ensure that your real estate investment is in good condition with no hidden issues that may be expensive to correct.

### *The Contractor*

The most important step in selecting a contractor is ensuring that he or she has all the proper trade licenses and insurance policies, and can prove it with current documentation. He or she must be bondable and have on-the-job insurance. You also want a contractor who can give you a reasonable and realistic completion time. Ask for referrals from other jobs and then call them all; you want to ensure that your property benefits from the skills of a qualified and professional contractor.

When you contact these referrals, ask if the contractor applied for all necessary permits to ensure that the work was legally done to local municipal and building code standards. If these sources are unsure, it is likely that the contractor did not get permits. It is also likely that the contractor won't be applying for the proper permits in doing your job.

No matter which contractor you hire, always confirm that these permits are obtained and the work is in compliance with them. At each stage of the job, ask to view the relevant permit and compare it to what was done.

All quotes should be given with material and labor costs itemized separately. This allows you to see exactly what you are paying for, making it easier to identify if you are being

overcharged. Don't hesitate to ask about the receipts for materials used in the project; an honest, professional contractor will be happy to show them to you.

Use your network of contacts to find a contractor with several years of experience who can recognize and advise you on potential dangers or problems with the property.

### The Insurance Agent

An experienced, astute insurance agent will arrange for reasonable insurance premiums on all your investment properties. He or she will also explain each type of policy, outline the differences, and make recommendations about which ones best suit your needs.

Finding an agent with many years of directly related experience is important because this gives him or her greater familiarity with the advantages and disadvantages of different features and policies. This level of insight will work to your greatest advantage. He or she will know, from experience, which insurance would be best for each type of investment property you own.

### The Appraiser

Real estate appraisers are specialists in estimating the market value of different investments, such as commercial and residential buildings and land. Insightful, competent appraisers produce a detailed report that includes a written description of the property and an estimate of its value based on meticulous analysis. Such appraisals are used when property is bought, sold, insured, or mortgaged. Independent-fee appraisers may also give expert testimony in court.

Their worth to you lies in their ability to determine the fair market value of your prospective investment, backing up their conclusions with factual information and a competent knowledge of the three appraisal methods described in Chapter Seven. As with the other members of your success team, experience and professionalism are very important. The appraiser's ability to identify and address unusual features or qualities of a property, and dedication to a thorough evaluation, are crucial to the accuracy of the appraisal.

He or she will assess a property and the neighborhood in which it is situated and validate its legally recorded description. This may include measuring and drawing land diagrams, noting the condition and special features of buildings, and determining legal road access. The property value will be estimated, citing governmental sources and local sales data.

With revenue-generating properties, an appraiser will also examine the income records and operating costs and estimate building replacement costs. All this gathered data is analyzed and evaluated, and a written report outlines the methods by which the fair market value was estimated.

## Rick's Success Strategy

Most successful investors will tell you that networking is one of the most important marketing tactics for growing your investment portfolio. It is about making connections and building mutually beneficial relationships. By making contact with different people or groups, you can benefit from their knowledge and expose yourself to a wide variety of investment opportunities. I believe that, to be successful as an investor, you must continually meet new people, build new relationships, and actively leverage the contacts in your network.

Creating a positive and lasting first impression with the people you meet in your network can open a lot of doors. Even networking with people who do not share the same interests can still bring you business. Most people have their own contacts and I have found that, even if they are not interested in what you have to offer, they often know someone who is. An important fact to remember when building a strong, successful network is the opportunities that come from knowing a diversity of people.

In getting to know other investors, you can also benefit from their experience. Investing is always a learning process and, while networking with other people, you may receive some advice that helps you to become more successful.

When I'm attending group meetings or functions, I always make a point of exchanging contact information and/or business cards. It's important to keep in touch with the contacts you have developed, so be sure to follow up with them. It is also crucial to create and maintain a database of all the contacts in your network. I always include their names, phone numbers, and email addresses as well as the date and location where I met them. This database allows me to stay in touch with the people in my network, pass along their names to others, and learn about promising investment opportunities and strategies.

Remember, however, that networking is about giving and taking. Be active in supporting others by sharing your knowledge, or the names of contacts that might have an interest in another person's services. If you want to benefit from the assistance of more experienced investors and utilize their contacts, you must also do your part.

# Chapter Nine

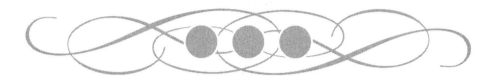

## *Building Your Assets:*

### POWERFUL PROPERTY AND TENANT MANAGEMENT

Now that you are in the business of real estate investing, you will quickly come to realize that there are some aspects you enjoy, others you would rather not bother with, and there will never be a time when you can do all of it yourself. Look for opportunities to offload responsibilities, such as property and tenant management. At first, you might need to do this work yourself. However, as soon as possible, you should consider delegating these duties to professionals who are specifically trained in this area.

If you are serious about creating wealth through real estate investing, learn to delegate. This is an important part of developing your mindset for success. Hiring skilled specialists to perform the tasks they excel in means that you can grow your real estate investment portfolio that much faster. It is important to identify your strengths and hire other professionals to support your goals with their talents.

Some investors enjoy the rush of locating, analyzing, and negotiating potential opportunities but fall apart when it comes to resulting paperwork and management. Others enjoy personally managing their portfolio and handling the day-to-day paperwork that comes with it, but this can consume the time needed to grow their wealth. No matter how you spend your time, keep your efforts focused on achieving your overall goal.

Remember that you are using our successful, proprietary strategy to develop your expertise as an investor. This includes understanding that your primary role is to identify, analyze, and acquire new properties. These very specialized skills require your commitment of time and effort. Free up your time by strategically delegating tasks to other experts. You will still need to lead your success team but it doesn't mean that you have to do everything.

## Property Management

Many people balk at property management because, when things are going smoothly, they can't justify paying a property management fee to someone who seemingly just collects rent each month. What they don't realize is the cost of not hiring a manager. By doing the work yourself, you many save on cash up front, but there is a price involved in directly managing your own properties.

What about the times when things do not go smoothly with the maintenance, repair, or tenant management of your properties? Resolving such issues takes valuable time away from the work of growing your portfolio. Unless you plan to get into the business yourself, it may be in your best interest to leave property management to an individual or company who specializes in it.

Property managers are experts at the myriad responsibilities that come with their profession. They understand the relevant landlord and tenant legislation and other important laws, have the experience to prevent problems from occurring, and can be very efficient in acting when things get a little bumpy. In addition, they have the teams and resources in place to keep your property effectively tenanted, which is something else you may not be as good at.

You will have to decide whether to manage your own portfolio or sign contracts with local property management companies. If you are just getting started, you may want to do it yourself; it will give you a feel for what's involved. But as your portfolio grows, or you begin investing outside your surrounding area, you will eventually require the services of a reliable property management company.

The advantages of using property managers include:

- they likely have much more experience in managing rental properties than you do;

- you do not have to deal directly with tenants;

- they make it possible to invest "out of town";

- they handle the daily maintenance and hassles that may arise;

- reputable property managers are experienced at interpreting the relevant landlord, tenant, and property laws;

- lenders have more confidence in your deal when they see that you intend to put a professional management company in charge, especially if you do not have this experience.

The disadvantages of using property managers include:

- they are paid based on gross income and may not manage the bottom line properly, which is about net income;

- there is a higher potential for theft, especially if rents are paid in cash;

- they will not be as diligent at keeping the building in good shape as you would;

- they will never dedicate the energy to your property that you would.

Your time is valuable; focus on doing the things that bring you the greatest potential for success. If you are skilled at locating profitable investment properties and acquiring joint venture partners to secure those properties, then invest most of your time doing just that. An experienced and reputable property manager enables you to spend your time acquiring even more investments.

**Leslie's Family Lesson**

I have personally chosen to use established and professional local property managers for all of my investments. My family has been investing in real estate for years and we came to realize that we could grow our portfolio more quickly and efficiently by delegating our property management needs to those who specialize in it.

There can be months when things run smoothly, but all it takes is one or two bad months with problem tenants to realize that hiring an experienced and reputable property manager is money well spent. We own some properties in transitional areas that require very strong management, and the fee we pay has been well worth it. It allows us to concentrate on our goal: growing our portfolio and real estate investment business.

In the early days, my father and his business partner managed their own portfolio. Although they may have saved money by doing so, they spent an equivalent amount, and then some, in terms of their time. In addition, because of their personalities and skill sets, it wasn't always easy for them to deal with tenants, especially when it came to evictions. Things that could have been taken care of fairly quickly tended to drag on.

In hindsight, it is obvious that their time would have been better spent focusing on those things they were good at. Having a few extra dollars coming directly to them at the end of each month wasn't worth the pain of all the day-to-day hassles.

Here are some things to keep in mind about property managers. First, if you decide to hire one, take the time to shop around. Thoroughly interview several potential companies to determine their experience and professional attitude. Ask for references, and then call them to ensure that the company is reputable and gather feedback about how well they managed other properties.

Second, no matter who you hire, remember to always stay on top of your property management company. They are often managing several properties and your needs may fall between the cracks. As with anything else, you must lead your team and ensure that they are meeting your expectations on how your property should be managed.

### Good Tenanting Tactics

Start viewing your tenants as clients. After all, they are paying you a substantial amount of money each month in exchange for housing. To retain quality tenants, treat them with respect and be sure to address their needs in a timely manner.

Attract the best tenants with creative marketing, such as offering incentives or advertising in unique venues. There will often be other rental units available that are similar to yours, so find a way to stand out from the crowd. We offer a $100 bonus with the signing of a one-year lease in our advertising for a residential rental. This attracts a lot of attention.

Take plenty of time to screen your potential tenants thoroughly. Vacancies are unavoidable; your reserve fund should be planned with this in mind to give you the time to carefully select a terrific replacement. From the first contact over the phone to showing the property and completing a rental application to the credit screening and approval process, be sure to actively evaluate your candidate's attitude with respect to appearance, punctuality, and professionalism. It is better to invest in placing a quality tenant in your unit than to jump at the first application.

At the end of the day, these are your properties and it is up to you to ensure that they are all managed well. Therefore, be up-to-date on the local landlord-tenant act and understand your rights and the rights of your tenants.

### Leslie's Tenant Troubles

Over the course of your real estate investing journey, you will inevitably have major challenges with some of your tenants. As you begin to build your network and compare notes with other investors, you will quickly realize that you're not alone in dealing with what seemed like unique issues. Eventually, you may feel like a soldier swapping war stories. While they will seem funny in hindsight, at the time they can seem insurmountable. The key is to persevere rather than throw your hands in the air and accept defeat.

I have had my fair share of trouble with tenants. I am extremely grateful to have hired experienced, accountable property managers who handle the day-to-day issues with my portfolio. But as the owner, it is sometimes necessary to directly handle the bigger problems.

A host of problems, and some wonderful lessons, came along with the first property I purchased outside of my province. It was the side-by-side duplex in Edmonton, Alberta that we discussed in Chapter Six. During my visit, I looked at several properties, analyzed them, spoke to the few people I knew in the area, and then took the plunge and put in my offer—far too quickly, as it turned out.

The vendor was offering some attractive seller financing. The property seemed structurally solid and in decent condition. There were already tenants in place, which I thought was a bonus: rental income coming in right away. It all looked great on the surface, and I didn't dig much deeper than that. In hindsight, I made many mistakes with this transaction. On a positive note, I have used the lessons I learned to become a much more astute investor.

First, I should not have rushed into things without doing more research. In an effort to get in my offer on what seemed to be an exceptional deal, I overlooked several important steps. These may seem like common sense, especially when investing in a property that was nowhere near where I live. But the clock was ticking down to my scheduled flight home, I got caught up in the rush of things, and I moved forward much more quickly than I normally would have.

Second, I should have spoken to a lot more people to get advice about the location. After my closing, I began growing my network of fellow investors in Alberta. From talking with these investors, as well as some new team members (the new property managers, my lawyer in Alberta, and the insurance agent I chose to work with in Alberta), I soon realized that the area was in transition and still extremely rough. It was definitely not the greatest location for investing.

Third, I made a big mistake by taking on existing tenants without thoroughly checking them out, including their payment history and references. The allure of being able to purchase a property that was already rented was soon replaced by a sinking feeling that the current tenants would be causing me a lot of grief.

Soon after my closing, the property manager informed me that the tenants in Unit One were causing a lot of problems and neighbors were complaining. Within a month of acquiring the property, we had begun the process of having them evicted. Throughout this ordeal, they were rude and belligerent, even resorting to insulting and racial remarks about my property manager.

We eventually evicted them, but the property was left in a horrible state. We faced major repairs and cleanup before we could even show it. And then, a few weeks after it went vacant, the detached garage burned to the ground. Although it was covered by insurance, we had quite a hassle getting everything cleaned up and orderly again. Today, I can laugh at all this; however, on the day I learned that the garage had burned down, I thought I was going to have a heart attack.

The tenants in Unit Two were more pleasant to deal with but seemed to be going through a lot of personal and financial problems. They were also very rough on the property; whenever I flew out for a visit, they would apologize for their mess and claim that they hadn't had time that day for cleaning. At the back of my mind, I wondered if, in the whole time they lived there, they'd ever fully cleaned the unit—it was that bad! There was definitely no pride of ownership. The only good thing was that they were responsive to our property manager and always gave advance notice if they would have problems making their rent payment.

Perhaps this doesn't seem like too bad a story, but there's more. The tenants in Unit Two had subleased the basement apartment to a recovering meth addict whose drug problems did not seem to be in check. He'd already had several run-ins with the police; eventually, they came to arrest him. With the house surrounded and nowhere to run, he decided that blocking the door with his coffee table was a great idea. So the police threw a flash-bomb through the window and knocked the door down with a battering ram. The good news is they removed him from my property. The bad news is my basement suite ended up looking like a war zone.

Today, there are still challenges but the property has settled down considerably since we purchased it. Had I walked away from all that turmoil, I would probably have lost money and ended up with a bad taste in my mouth about real estate investing. Instead, I chose to view it as a series of extremely valuable lessons that I needed to learn to become a better investor.

You may wonder why I share this story in a book about successful real estate investing. The answer is because all successful people make mistakes, and fail, and occasionally act on impulse. The key is they don't allow themselves to be defeated; they learn the necessary lessons and then keep going.

**Build the Value of Your Asset**

Because real estate is a physical asset that can be improved in different ways, you can better control its value compared to other investments. By talking with investors, contractors, and other real estate professionals, you will learn many techniques for enhancing residential and commercial property.

Start by increasing the income-producing potential. Understand the needs of your clients (your tenants) and carefully reposition your property for higher rents. This includes strategic marketing to attract a different clientele. Offering a well-managed, attractive property can help you to command a higher rental rate than comparable units in the area.

Also maximize the physical use of your property. As we discussed in Chapter Six, creating a basement apartment is one example of turning open space into additional revenue-generating areas. Walk through every part of a property to see what space is unused or underused, and think creatively about what you can do with it. In commercial properties or apartment buildings, you can rent interior space as storage areas or turn a ground floor section into retail space.

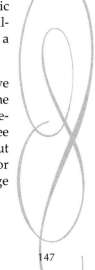

Physical enhancements to increase the overall value include cosmetic repairs and careful renovations. But this needs to be done strategically with good planning. Read below for Rick's discussion on this subject.

**Rick's Value-Adding Renovation Strategy**

Whether your goal is a short-term fix-and-flip or a longer-term hold, there are many ways you can improve the value of your property. However, when it comes to renovations, it is best to stay with basic cosmetic enhancements. Otherwise, I believe it is unlikely that you'll get back the return you desire on your investment.

For example, to increase your rents on a residential property, the simplest strategy is to freshen the appearance with cosmetic repairs to help it show well. Then, with astute marketing, you will attract quality tenants who are looking for a nice place to live. If, however, you try to upgrade further by putting in luxury features, it will take several years to recoup that investment.

Consider the cost of installing a $5,000 Jacuzzi bathtub. While it will definitely add a luxurious touch, when you consider the rental increase you can reasonably expect, you'll find that you are spending a lot of dollars to attract a higher paying tenant.

Whether you are buying and holding a property for one year, five years, or ten years, it is advisable to locate houses that only require cosmetic makeovers. As an investor, I generally prefer properties that are easiest and cheapest to repair, located in areas that can maximize my return when I sell them.

Look for houses that will need simple things, such as a good cleanup with fresh paint, floor tiles, or carpet; minor wall repairs; and a yard cleared of garbage or overgrown plants. Such houses will not appeal to most buyers, but experienced investors will spot these properties as potential gold mines. They don't see what the property looks like at the time it's purchased but will visualize the polished, finished product.

A simple renovation plan can lead you into a very smart and profitable investment. As we discussed in Chapter Six, it is essential for you to carefully develop a repair-cost plan and budget, focusing on the areas that will increase value the most. When renovated and modernized, the kitchen and bathrooms (including master bedroom en suites) offer the most potential for enhancing the resale value of a house.

Adding garages, family rooms, and bedrooms are popular and potentially profitable additions. But you must carefully evaluate whether you can recover the expense of doing all this work. To maximize my return on an investment property, I always avoid doing unnecessary upgrades or repairs that only add cost to the renovation but do not increase the home's value.

If I am considering an investment in buy, fix, and sell real estate, or "flipping" a house, to understand what will maximize my profit, it is beneficial to start with the location. I take my time learning the market in the surrounding area. I do comparables for houses that have sold nearby, looking carefully at how long they took to sell. This allows me to spot a good deal when I see it and calculate length of time it might take to resell it.

Many experienced real estate investors can make millions of dollars by turning ugly houses into beautiful homes. However, inexperienced investors often lose money this way because they overpay for the house or underestimate the costs involved. These include construction costs, carrying costs during the renovation (mortgage payments, utilities, property tax, etc.), lawyers' and realtors' fees for the purchase and sale, closing costs, and possible capital-gains tax. They all must be factored into your repair-cost budget because they greatly affect the profitability of a potential investment.

If you are just beginning to build your real estate portfolio, you must always remember your limitations. It is crucial to have your investment property inspected and complete every step of your due diligence. Use a great deal of caution when considering property that requires major structural repairs or has problems with leaky basements or mold. These repairs can be very costly and turn your property into an investment nightmare.

If you are considering the purchase of an investment property with major repair issues, it is always best to get written estimates from several reliable contractors. Hire only experienced professionals to do these critical repairs. Always take all costs into account before deciding on whether or not to purchase the property.

*Chapter Ten*

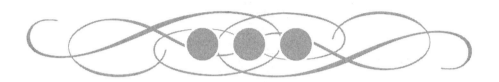

*Generational Legacy:*

MANAGING AND GROWING YOUR WEALTH FOREVER

*"Sow a thought, and you reap an act;*
*Sow an act, and you reap a habit;*
*Sow a habit, and you reap a character;*
*Sow a character, and you reap a destiny."*
— Charles Reade

No matter where you are in the adventure, you must always move forward to be a truly successful investor. It is absolutely critical to not lose your momentum. As business coach Tony Robbins says, "The most important thing you can do to achieve your goals is to make sure that as soon as you set them, you immediately begin to create momentum… never leave the site of setting a goal without first taking some form of positive action toward its attainment."

If you are just getting started in real estate investing, as soon as you develop a thorough understanding of the basics, begin implementing them. Keep the energy up: apply the principles outlined in our proprietary strategy to acquire your first property and then continuously work to build your portfolio. Remember to "think big" and set extraordinary goals that will motivate you; this is an important factor in your mindset for success.

If you already own investment properties, your focus must now be divided. You should be creating and supervising the team that acquires and manages your investments while you actively research your next purchase. Setting a dynamic pace, balanced between these two important actions, is the key to continuously growing your wealth. You must ensure that you always have quality tenants in place; carefully select a winning administrative team; and then step back from the day-to-day tasks to focus on building your portfolio.

Be sure to keep up the momentum of taking action, no matter how small, toward your goals. Action doesn't necessarily mean going out and purchasing property every month. It can be as simple as building your skills by taking another course; joining a networking group; meeting with team members or fellow investors; or just doing research on different geographical areas and analyzing potential properties.

The point is to steadily move forward. It's the culmination of these little steps that brings you closer to achieving your personal dream. Successful people carefully prepare themselves by honing their skills. But when the time comes to take action, they don't hesitate. So once you get your momentum up, be sure to keep at it every day. Remember that you will inevitably make mistakes; view each one as a learning experience, use your newly acquired knowledge to modify your approach, and keep going.

We've been repeating the idea of continuously focusing on your goals. That's because we live in a world where the "scarcity mentality" is so prevalent that many people focus on making excuses for not having the wealth that others do while resenting those who actively take control of their lives, their wealth, and their destinies. Don't limit yourself like this; believe in what you can accomplish, set big goals, and take action toward achieving them. Soon, those seemingly distant dreams will become your delightful reality.

By choosing to create wealth through real estate investing, you are naturally stepping into a leadership role. The rat race is no longer satisfactory and you are actively searching for a better solution. Remember, however, that this choice comes with certain responsibilities. It is up to you to lead the team you select to acquire investments and manage your portfolio.

That team must also include your family members. Invest time in educating your family on the essentials of wealth creation and wealth management. This is an important component in protecting the legacy you create. The same goes for estate planning; it should begin right from the start. Remember that, although you might be at the beginning of your journey, your goal is to have the lifestyle of your dreams. With the end result in mind, start acting today to build—and protect—your wealth.

## Leslie Keeps Up Her Momentum

When I first got started with real estate investing, I set a goal of acquiring one property a year. But the thrill and pride I felt after closing my first investment was soon replaced by a never-ending itch to do more. I could have waited until the next year to secure my second property, but I decided to keep moving forward. Two more properties went into my portfolio that first year.

There's an abundance of opportunities if you open your eyes to the possibilities. It's amazing what you can accomplish by setting high standards while using the momentum created from steady, daily action.

The funny thing is, I spent months eagerly anticipating the closing on my first property. But when the day came, it felt just like any other day. There were no fireworks; there was only a sudden, compelling eagerness to move onto the next project as soon as possible!

That's when I realized that the fun is in the journey. For me, the challenge of continuing to build my portfolio while helping others to create their own wealth is truly my passion. A huge reason why Rick and I have written this book is to share our personal experiences with investing as a way of encouraging and motivating others to start their own journey.

When you find a group of like-minded individuals who share your passion, the synergy can be amazing. Rick and I work together every day and the energy in our office is phenomenal because we share an enthusiasm for growing our real estate investment portfolios and our businesses.

My parents always taught me to think big and encouraged me to develop the mindset that nothing is impossible. From their example I learned to not focus or dwell on problems but to be solution oriented. After acquiring my first three properties, I felt great pride in my accomplishment. But to live the lifestyle of my dreams, I knew there was a lot of work ahead. The great part is that, because I enjoy what I do, it never really feels like work.

I have had the pleasure of meeting hundreds of other like-minded investors who share my passion. I think that the synergy that has ensued from surrounding myself with so many positive, passionate, and successful real estate investors gave me the push I needed to move forward at a pace I never thought I could sustain.

I recently moved into acquiring commercial real estate, with plans to grow this portion of my portfolio exponentially over the next few years. My first commercial purchase came after I had spent more than a year intensely learning about this sector. I invested time and money into appropriate courses;

spoke with other investors who were actively investing in commercial real estate; and spent endless hours doing my own research, both online and by reading relevant books.

The challenge for me now is to effectively delegate and oversee the tasks necessary to manage my existing portfolio. This will give me the time to actively seek out new commercial opportunities and put appropriate structures in place for acquiring them.

We all have different goals and objectives for our lives. Our different upbringings, cultures, and ways of thinking mean that the manner in which we go about creating wealth varies with each of us. But our common bond is an interest in real estate. Some of you, like me, may be passionate about the real estate investment industry. Others may see real estate investment as a good, but passive, part of their portfolio. In either case, determine what you are passionate about and let it drive you to create the wealth you need to start living your dreams today.

## Create Long-Term, Intergenerational Wealth

Building a solid, profitable real estate investment portfolio allows you to create long-term wealth that can be passed on from generation to generation. The investment decisions you make today can give your family a solid financial foundation to expand upon. But no one lives forever. So you should think of your portfolio as your legacy, providing for your loved ones long after you are gone.

Set up a well-managed, profitable real estate investment portfolio and then educate your family on the essentials of wealth creation and wealth management. It is important to involve your family because they must have the right mindset and knowledge to maintain and grow that portfolio. Why work so hard on creating wealth only to have it lost or squandered because your family lacks knowledge or an understanding of financial responsibility?

You can create a legacy of financial stability and also teach the financial literacy that ensures your family can skillfully build or rebuild wealth in the future. Knowledge and financial literacy are much more valuable than the actual real estate assets. The profitability of a portfolio is largely dependent on how well it is managed. Proper management can only come from experience and continuous education.

### Leslie's Advice about Estate Planning

It's easy to get caught up in the exhilaration of growing your business and expanding your portfolio. The creative process brings joyful energy to your life. As Pope Paul VI said, "Somebody should tell us, right at the start of our lives, that we are dying. Then we might live life to the limit, every minute of every day. Do it! I say. Whatever you want to do, do it now! There are only so many tomorrows."

Pope Paul VI suggests that we live life to the limit. Yet we must also plan for the future and the fact that we will all eventually die. Your success depends on vigorously pursuing your dreams. At the same time, ensure that you protect the result of your triumphant effort with a proper estate plan.

As you build your portfolio, continue working with your lawyers, accountants, and other team members to protect your wealth. They can advise you on the best way to hold your assets and structure your business. It is much easier to get it set up right the first time around than having to react to unexpected circumstances that will arise in the future.

Estate planning will be a critical part of this process. It will protect your assets and minimize unnecessary expenses, taxes, and so forth.

Ideally, you want your team members working together, advising you and taking the time to explain their reasoning. However, you will sometimes get contradictory information from your team. For example, a lawyer will look at things from

156

a liability perspective whereas an accountant will look at the tax issues. Sometimes these two points of view will be complementary while at other times they will conflict.

Just take it all in, review the information, ask questions, and then decide how you want to proceed. They may be experts in their chosen fields, but you are the one who truly cares about your portfolio. Remember that it is up to you to lead your team.

Over the years, you will spend a lot of time and effort building and managing your portfolio so it is essential that you also take time to protect what you have built. An estate plan is an essential element in creating a lasting legacy for generations to come. This process of outlining and organizing your finances should begin right from the start.

Many people assume that estate planning is only for the rich, or something to be concerned with only after your have accumulated wealth. However, proper estate planning is important regardless of where you are in your life and your current financial status.

An estate plan defines how your assets will be divided when you are gone; without it, the government decides what to do after your death. By predetermining this, you take control of your estate by planning ahead to minimize potential taxes and chart a smoother, more efficient transfer of your assets to family members. A proper estate plan also defines what happens should you become unable to manage your personal affairs due to illness.

Although thinking about your demise isn't the most pleasant activity, it is inevitable. You can't take your material wealth with you, so the best thing you can do is have your affairs in order for your family. A clear outline of your wishes makes it easier for them at a time when they are mourning your loss. It also reduces family tension and arguments.

Find a reputable estate planning lawyer to work with your lawyers and accountants and ensure that you have all your bases covered. In addition, get your family involved in the process so they understand what you are doing and how it all works. Once you have an estate plan in place, remember to review it and make updates as your situation changes. Your life is constantly moving, changing directions as you grow, so it will be a continual process.

In summary, make sure to keep taking action. Take advantage of the momentum you've created and go with it. Just like a snowball, it takes work to get it all rolling, but once you're steadily moving ahead it takes a lot less effort to grow that snowball. Whether it's looking at and analyzing properties, putting in offers, building relationships, or continuously learning, the point is that you need to keep moving.

Your success depends on getting out of your comfort zone and taking action to set up a portfolio that works for you. Then you can begin to live your dreams today. So set new standards for yourself and then get going!

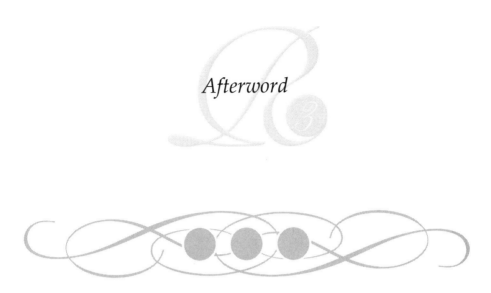

*Afterword*

## Final Thoughts

As our book draws to an end, we want to share some final thoughts on creating wealth with real estate. Regardless of education, financial background, or social status, every one of us has tremendous potential to achieve the success and wealth of our dreams. We can accomplish the goals we set for ourselves if we take steady, daily action to achieve those goals. Believe in this, and cultivate the mindset that is the foundation of your success.

To become a winning investor, find what you are passionate about and let it drive you to create the wealth you need to start living your dreams today. Begin by answering the important question: "What do I want to accomplish by investing in real estate?" Think about where you want to be in a year, five years, and ten years from now. Then use your answer to stay focused and guide your decisions.

You must clearly identify and document your goals and objectives. Work with our proprietary strategy to ensure that the investment properties and strategies you choose will lead to achieving those goals. Set timelines and milestones, track your progress, and motivate yourself toward greater success. Then implement your plan to accomplish the success you desire. Finally, know that what you desire you will achieve, regardless of the obstacles. These are the keys to your success.

We also recommend maintaining a longer-term perspective about investing. Creating true wealth is an ongoing process. It's not a get-rich-quick scheme. Unlike fix-and-flip real estate television shows, our successful proprietary strategy focuses on creating lasting wealth through investing. This means acquiring and keeping revenue-generating property with positive cash flow while skillfully managing your portfolio.

While short-term strategies (such as fixing and flipping houses) have their place, they focus on asset appreciation, which (as the U.S. market has shown) isn't very predictable. Anyone following that strategy should have a solid understanding of the specific market, a firm handle on the costs involved, and a good team to carry out the project.

Buying for cash flow can lead to more stable, long-term assets. The author of *Secrets of the Millionaire Mind*, T. Harv Eker, describes his commercial property as follows: "I'm not selling it, so I don't care if it's appreciating a million dollars, or five million dollars, or if it's going down a million dollars. I just get my same check every month. They still pay their rent. Their rent is the same every month. In fact, it's going to go up in about a year. I'm just looking for cash flow." Eker also predicts that, because of the cyclical nature of the real estate market, his assets will eventually go up in value. "It will go back up again. It's done that for a million years."

In most areas of the world, the economy is in the middle of a shakedown. With all the job losses, market corrections, and doom-and-gloom news reports, there are a lot of frightened people out there. Don't be one of them. Stay focused on your goal and go out in the world to find the opportunities that will help you to achieve your dreams. That's what sophisticated investors are doing right now.

From our experience as successful real estate investors, we have shared Canadian examples of an international process that achieves long-term results. You can use our step-by-step process to effectively evaluate any property located anywhere in the world. Cultivate your mindset for success and look for opportunities—they do exist, and many people are prospering right now.

Pursue your success by thinking like an entrepreneur. Be solution-oriented, treat your tenants like valued clients, develop well-defined exit strategies and critical planning as part of your joint ventures, and cultivate your creativity by thinking outside the box. Most importantly, persevere against all obstacles. That's how to become successful at anything you do, including real estate investing.

Support your success with a strong network of experts in accounting, real estate law, property management, and any other areas you need to help you do what you are best at: building your wealth through real estate investing. It is equally important to take the time to continuously educate yourself on how to create a lasting financial legacy that will grow exponentially.

Invest in the specific knowledge and tools you need to successfully locate, analyze, and secure profitable opportunities. Take courses and network to build your success tools. You can supplement these tools with seminars such as *Real Estate Fundamentals*, which expands on the principles outlined in this book while providing opportunities to meet other investors. Our hands-on practice in real estate investing, through working with genuine local examples and data, helps

our students to hone their skills. This is the kind of value-added instruction you want to look for.

We find that our students are eager to connect with each other and network to develop their ability to create wealth through real estate investing. So we also offer half-day workshops, which enable participants to meet new contacts and listen to local experts discuss topics such as accounting, construction, and government regulations. If this opportunity does not exist near you, then why not create it!

Remember to observe the highest standards for your performance as an investor. Ensure that your area studies, due diligence, and financial analysis are thoroughly professional, leading to the most astute choices when acquiring new property. Most of all, remember to take action.

The worst thing you can do is become paralyzed by fear—of the economy; of making a mistake; of not being worthy of the wealth you desire, or of whatever it is that could hold back your success. Surround yourself with winners: people who know how to find the prospect in every problem, who turn adversities into triumphs, and who encourage each other to keep their sights set on the goal. Let them inspire you, every day, to pursue your dreams and thrive with real estate investing.

Good luck! Never stop progressing toward your goals. With every achievement, remember to celebrate with your success team and then set the bar a bit higher for yourself. Eventually, a business magazine might add your name to their list of the 100 richest real estate investors in the world.

REAL PEOPLE *with* REAL STRATEGIES
*for* REAL ESTATE INVESTING

WWW.R3BOOK.COM

# R3 Glossary of Terms

**Agreement of Purchase and Sale:** Also known as an Offer to Purchase, this document is a legal contract by which one party agrees to sell, and another agrees to purchase, a property. When finalized, it binds both parties to its terms.

**Appreciation:** The increase in value of a property over time; it is influenced by many factors such as inflation, the economics of supply and demand, and capital improvements.

**Asset:** In real estate, this is property under ownership that has value.

**Balance Sheet:** It provides a snapshot of a company's financial position. The assets appear on the left, listed in the order in which they can be converted into cash. Liabilities appear on the right in the order they must be liquidated. The balance sheet shows whether the company is 'liquid' or whether it can effectively meet its short-term obligations, and the company's leverage (the ratio between capital lent by creditors and capital provided by its owners). The data reflect a fundamental accounting equation where Owners' Equity (or Net Worth) = Assets – Liabilities (or Net Assets).

**Capital:** Assets such as a sum of money that can be used to acquire or produce other assets.

**Cash Flow:** The difference of cash revenues less cash outlays over a given period of time. (excluding non-cash expenses).

**Cash-on-Cash Return:** The ratio of before-tax cash flow to the total amount of cash invested. The sum is expressed as a percentage. It is often used to evaluate the cash flow from income-producing properties but some use it to determine if a property is underpriced, indicating instant equity.

**Close; Closing Date:** The date specified in the Agreement of Purchase when the property will change ownership.

**Comparables:** Data about properties that are comparable in type and size to the one that is of interest to a buyer or a seller. This financial, and other, information can consist of previously sold properties as well as current listings.

**Debt Service:** A combination of the interest accruing on the mortgage and the actual repayment of the principal, or loan. At first, the largest portion of this payment will consist of interest, with a much smaller portion being principal reduction. Over time, as the amount owed shrinks, the reverse occurs: the bulk of the payment is applied toward the principal.

**Due Diligence:** A number of concepts involving the investigation of a business or person, or the performance of an act to specified standards. Commonly applied to voluntary investigations, it can also involve a legal obligation.

**Equity:** The difference between the market value of the property and the claims held against it.

**Foreclosure:** When an owner does not make the mortgage payments, and therefore defaults on a mortgage contract, the lender will repossess the property.

**Internal Rate of Return (IRR):** The gain or loss of an investment over a specified period, expressed as a percentage. While the actual rate of return of a given project will often differ from its estimated IRR rate, a project with a substantially higher IRR value than other available options would still provide a much better chance of strong growth.

**Joint Venture:** The partnership between two or more parties for the purpose of acquiring and developing real estate.

**Lien:** The claim placed by a creditor on a piece of real estate to ensure the payment of a debt.

**Leverage:** Strategic use of borrowed capital to increase the potential return of an investment.

**Portfolio:** The investment holdings of an investor or investment company.

**Principal:** Money originally invested or loaned. Interest rates and returns are calculated based on this amount.

**Profit and Loss Statement:** Also known as an income statement, this key financial statement is like a report card on a company's activities, presenting the net income or net loss relative to retained earnings from operations over a fiscal period. It includes calculations of gross income, operating income, and pre-tax income, which are crucial for analyzing a company's operations.

**ROI/Return on Investment:** The level of profit expected from the investment.

**Sweat Equity:** Labor used to build or improve a property and increase its equity.

**Tangible Asset:** A physical asset with intrinsic value, such as land or real estate.

**Tax Sale:** When a taxation authority forces a property to be auctioned to recover outstanding taxes.

**Upside Potential:** The potential price or gain that may be expected in a security or in a security average, generally stated as the dollar price or the dollar amount of gain that may reasonably be expected in the particular security or security average. For example, an analyst may feel that a stock currently selling at $25 per share has an upside potential of $40.

**Vendor-Take-Back Mortgage (VTB):** Where the seller will take back a portion of the mortgage, creating a secondary lien on the property. Also known as seller-financed deals.

# Recommended Resources

# **LEAH**SMALL

### REALTOR®

*Making Kitchener-Waterloo\* investors happy since 2001*

*\*and surrounding areas*

## INVESTMENT RESIDENTIAL PROPERTIES & COMMERCIAL REAL ESTATE

Leah Small
leahsmall@sympatico.ca
Office: (519) 885-0200
Toll-Free: 1-877-450-0200

RE/MAX Twin City Realty Inc., Brokerage
Independently Owned & Operated
83 Erb Street, Waterloo ON N2L 6C2

**59**% of Canadians said they'd be in financial trouble if their paycheque was delayed by even one week.

**33**% of respondents said they've been trying to save money,

while **42**% said they haven't been saving at all.

*"Even in a recession, the 'keeping up with the Joneses' ideal persists,* says Ken Hardy, professor emeritus of marketing at the University of Western Ontario's Richard Ivey School of Business. *'We don't give up lifestyle easily,'* he says. *"There's so much social pressure."'*

**Globe and Mail:** *Living hand to mouth* – Monday, September 14, 2009

**STAY AHEAD OF THE GAME AND INVEST WISELY
TO GET YOUR MONEY WORKING FOR YOU!**

INVEST with
Meridian Commercial Investments Inc.

Create a legacy of wealth and abundance!
Achieve financial freedom!
Live the life of your dreams today!

Providing steady income and long-term capital growth through joint commercial real estate investment opportunities.

MERIDIAN
Commercial Investments Inc.

**Contact us today
for more information:**

**(905) 467-6322**

*lquinsay@meridianinvestment.com*
www.meridianinvestment.com

# REAL ESTATE
## INVESTMENT SOLUTIONS

> "To invest successfully over a lifetime does not require stratospheric I.Q., unusual business insight or inside information. What is needed is a sound intellectual framework for making decisions and the ability to keep emotions from corroding that framework."
> **- Warren Buffet -**

# Create Wealth with Real Estate

At Real Estate Investment Solutions, our focus is on helping our investors reach their long-term financial goals by making their money work for them. We do this by providing real estate investment opportunities and strategies.

We specialize in identifying strong real estate opportunities and profitable investment opportunities for our clients

# Access to opportunities

We take time to understand your goals, investment style, and investment timelines. We actively seek out investments that would be suitable for your clients or pass on some of the excellent investment opportunities that come our way.

# Systems

We use a proven system to identify strong real estate investment opportunities. We diligently analyze every individual opportunity to make sure that it is a solid, profitable investment.

CONTACT US TODAY FOR MORE INFORMATION:
## (905) 317-3277
*rmckinnon@real-estateinvestmentsolutions.com*

# LOOMING PERSONAL
## *financial crisis!*

*"Canada's aging work force hasn't saved enough to retire. Pension benefits are being slashed, employees are working longer, the elderly are selling their homes and going back to work."*

**Globe and Mail:** *Retirement Dreams Under Siege*
– October 16, 2009
- *72% of Canadians say they do not have a financial plan.*
- *Average consumer in Canada has debt 22% higher than their income.*
- *50% of Canadians feel they are 1 or 2 pay-cheques away from a financial crisis.*

**National Post:** *Improving Canadian's Financial Literacy* – Wed, Jan 31, 2007

*Knowledge is Power!* Let Wealth and Business Academy guide you toward financial freedom by providing you with the tools and knowledge you need to start building a solid and profitable investment portfolio.

**PROMOTING FINANCIAL LITERACY AND A SUCCESS-ORIENTED MINDSET!**

WORKSHOPS – SEMINARS – BOOKS – EXPOS – HOME STUDY COURSES

CONTACT US TODAY FOR MORE INFORMATION:

**(905) 317-3277 or (905) 467-6322**

info@wbacademy.ca | www.wbacademy.ca